BYE BYE

PAPER

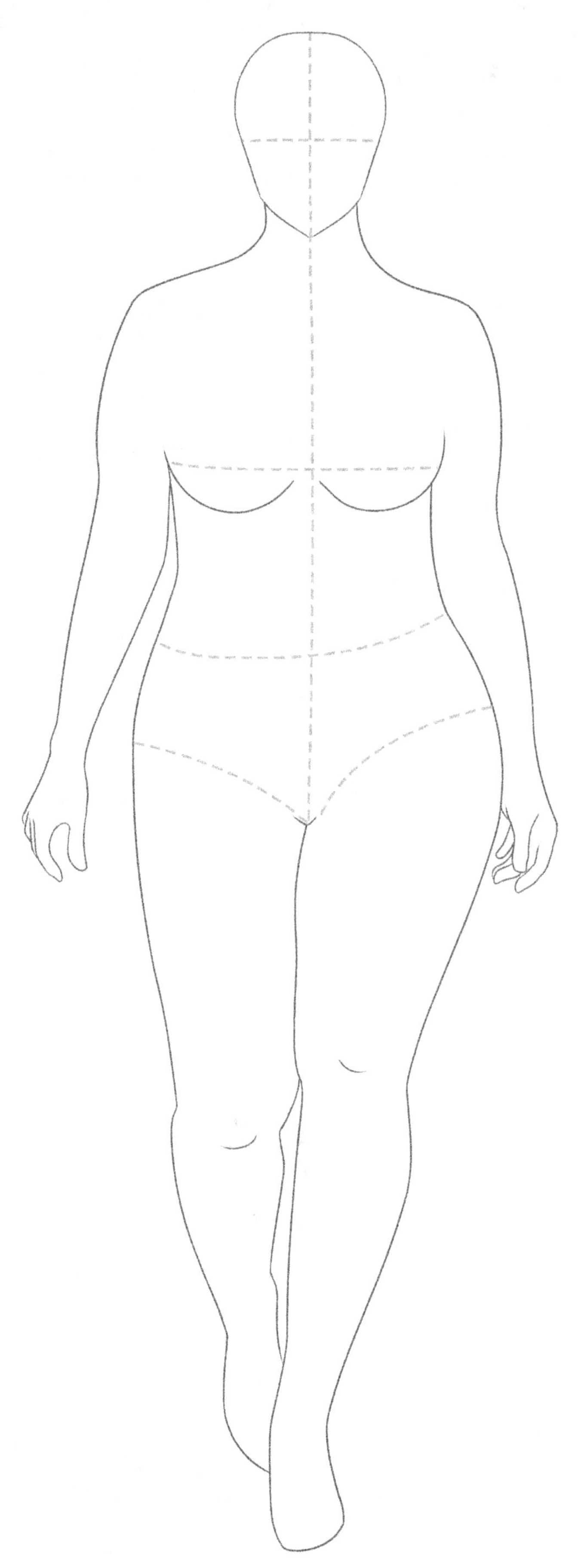

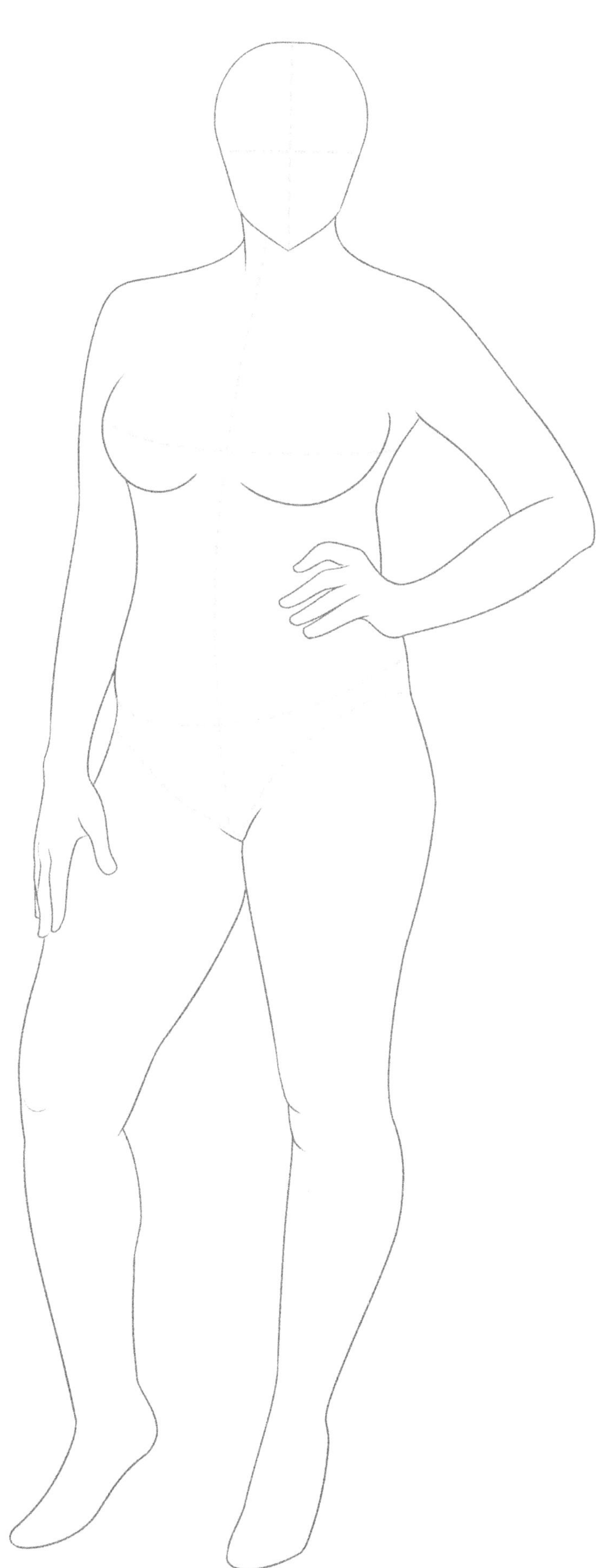

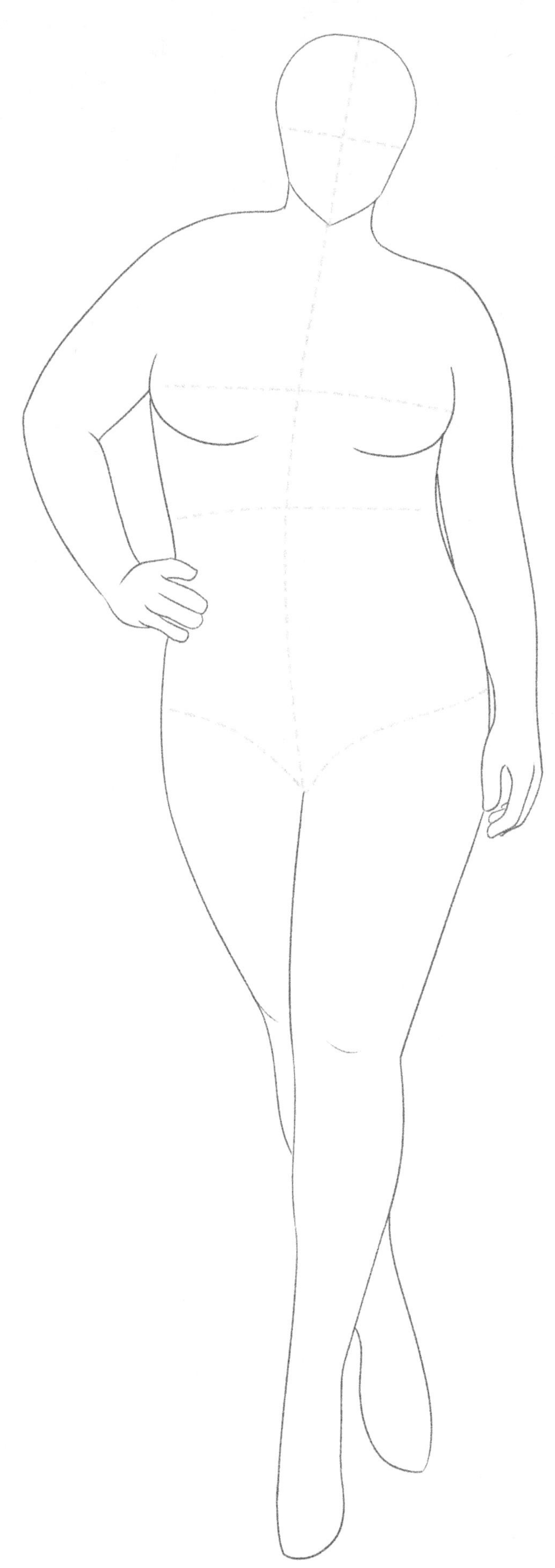

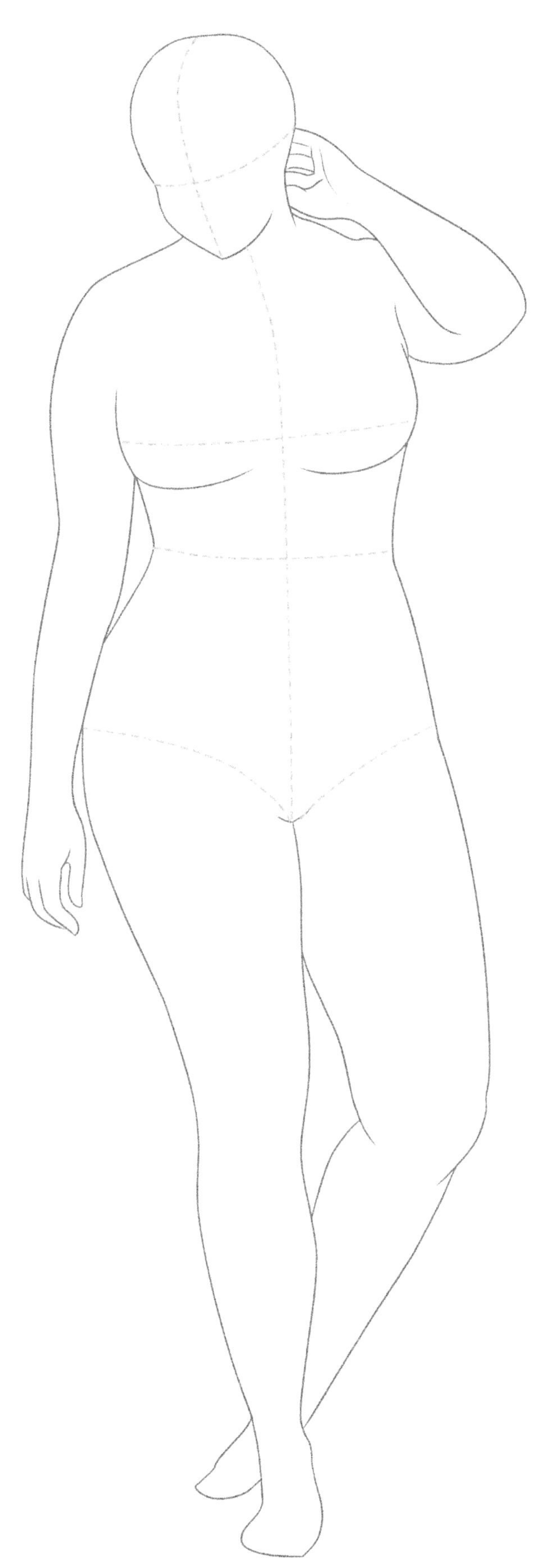

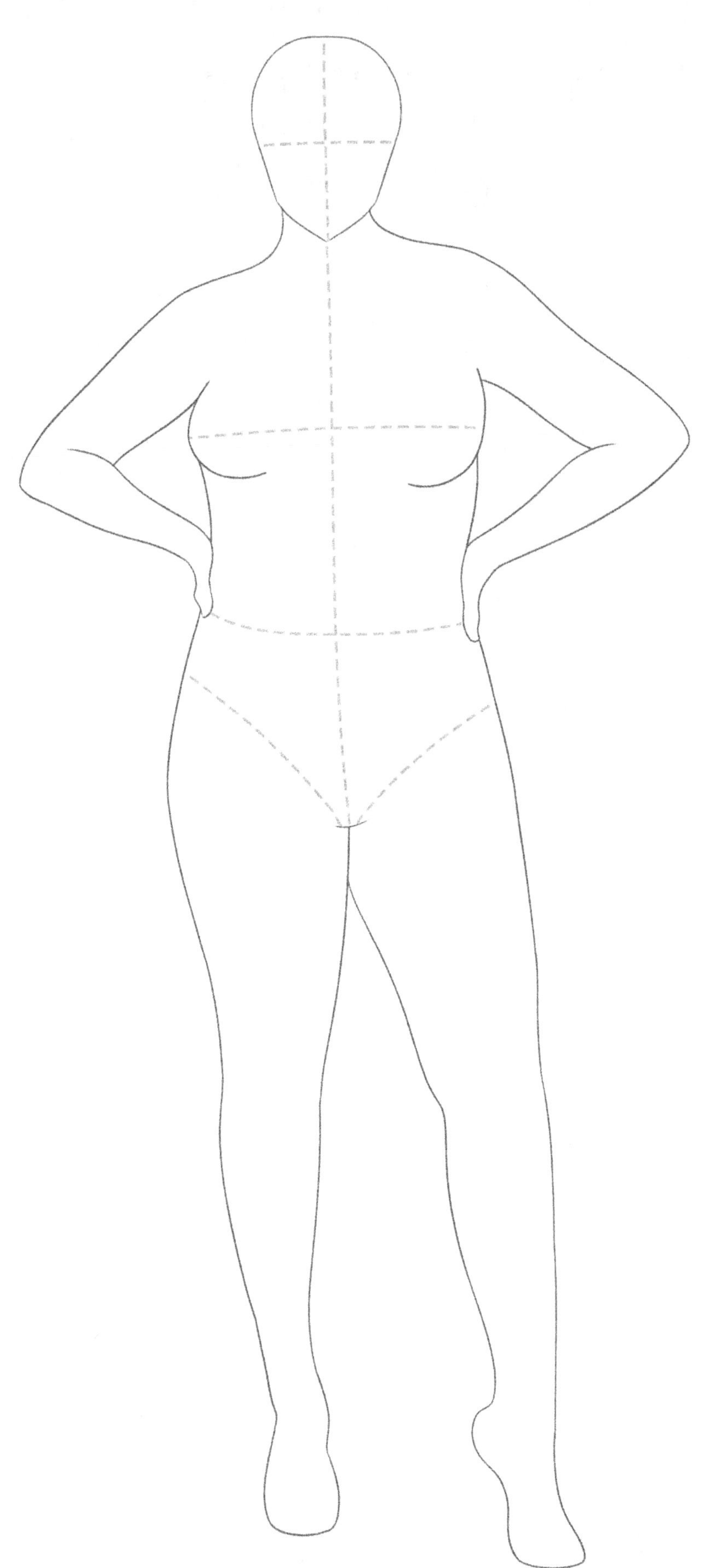

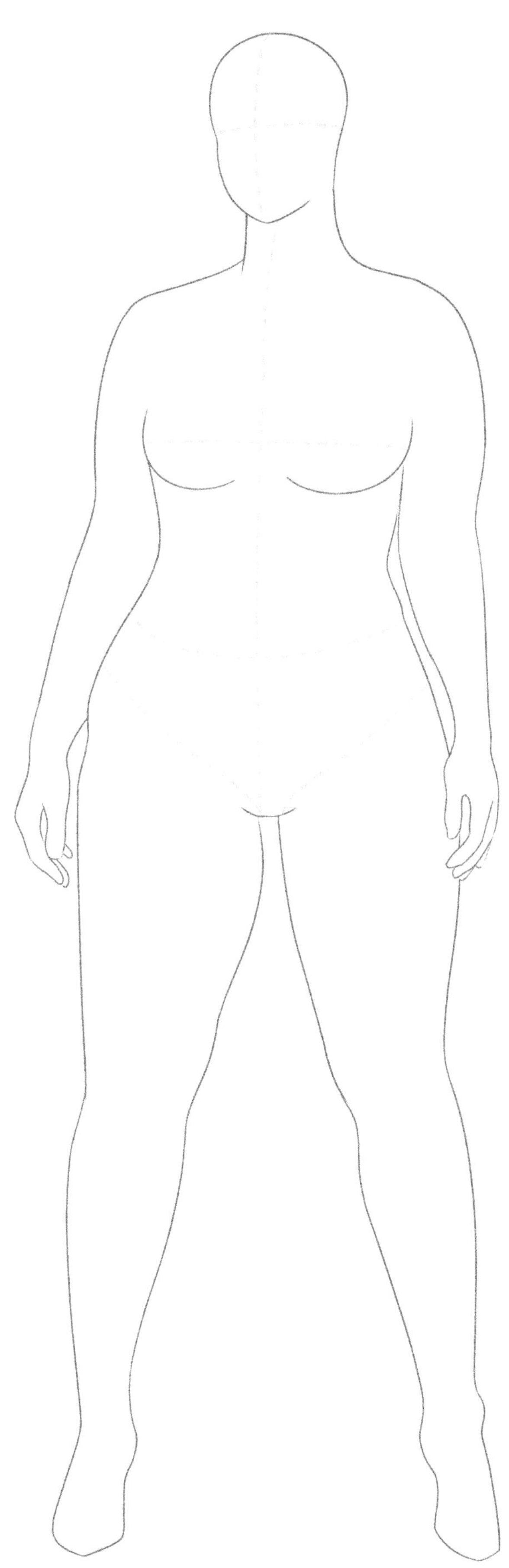

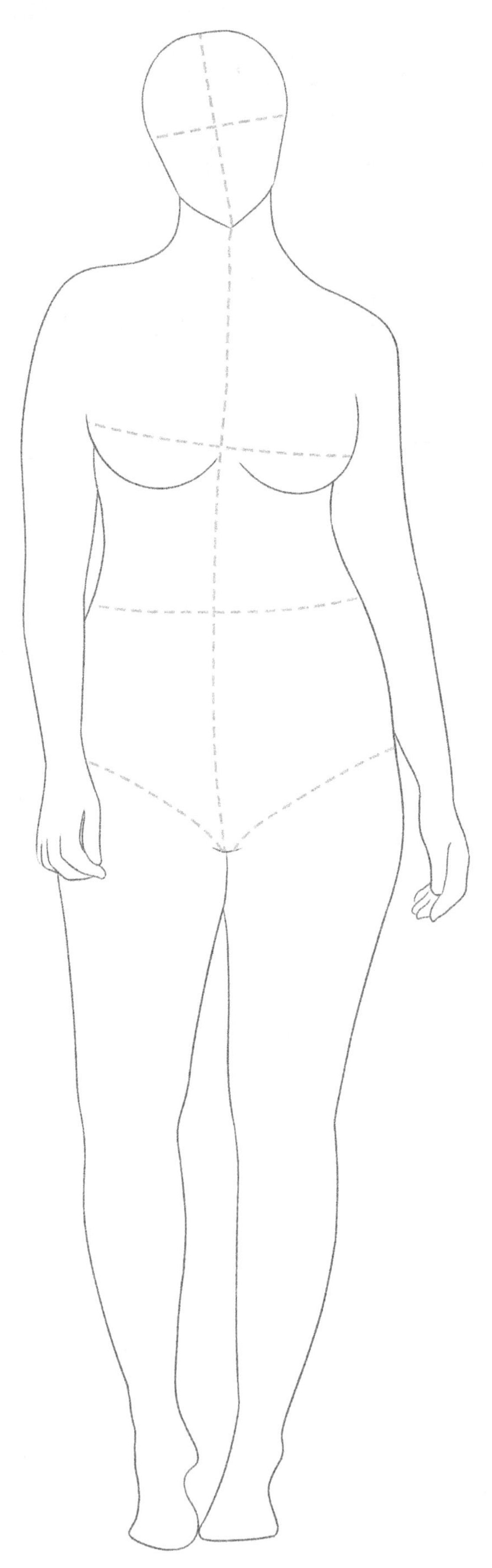

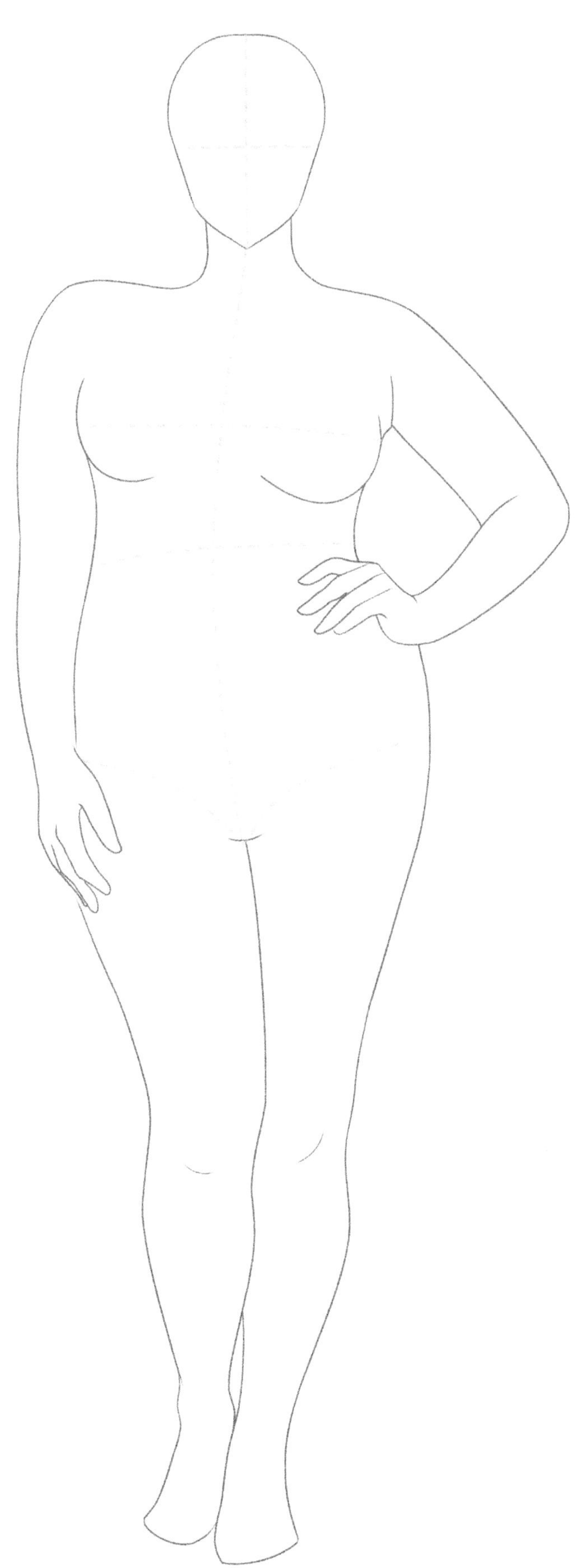

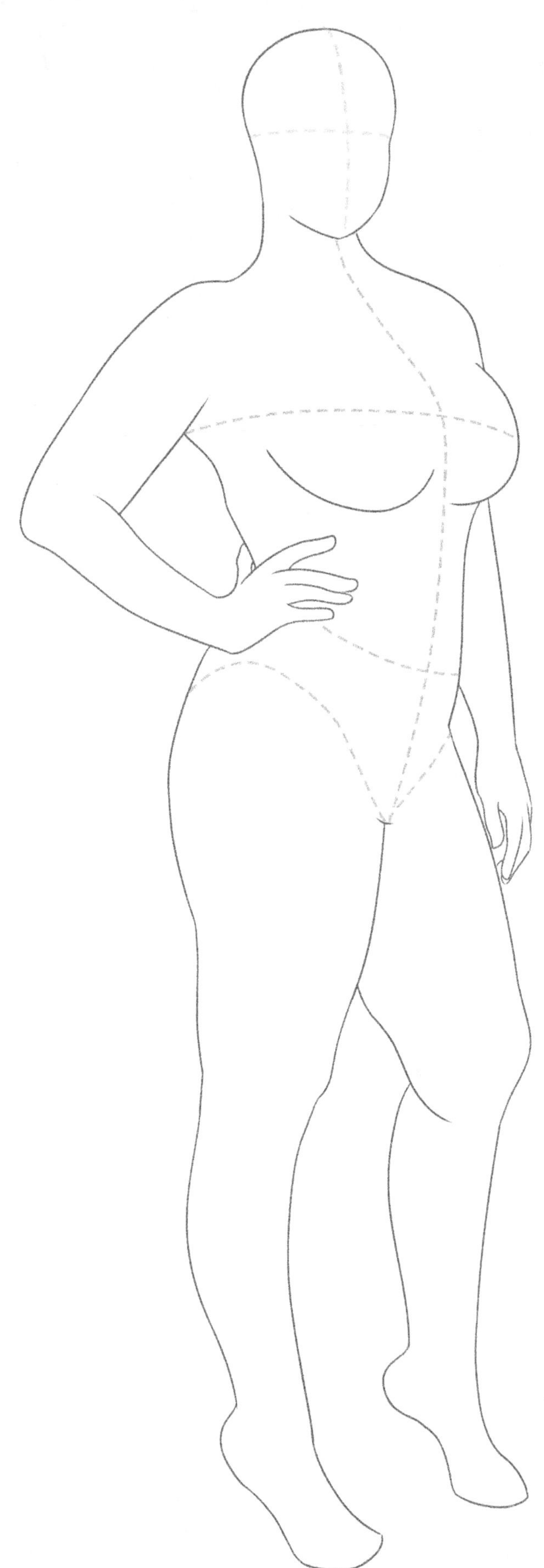

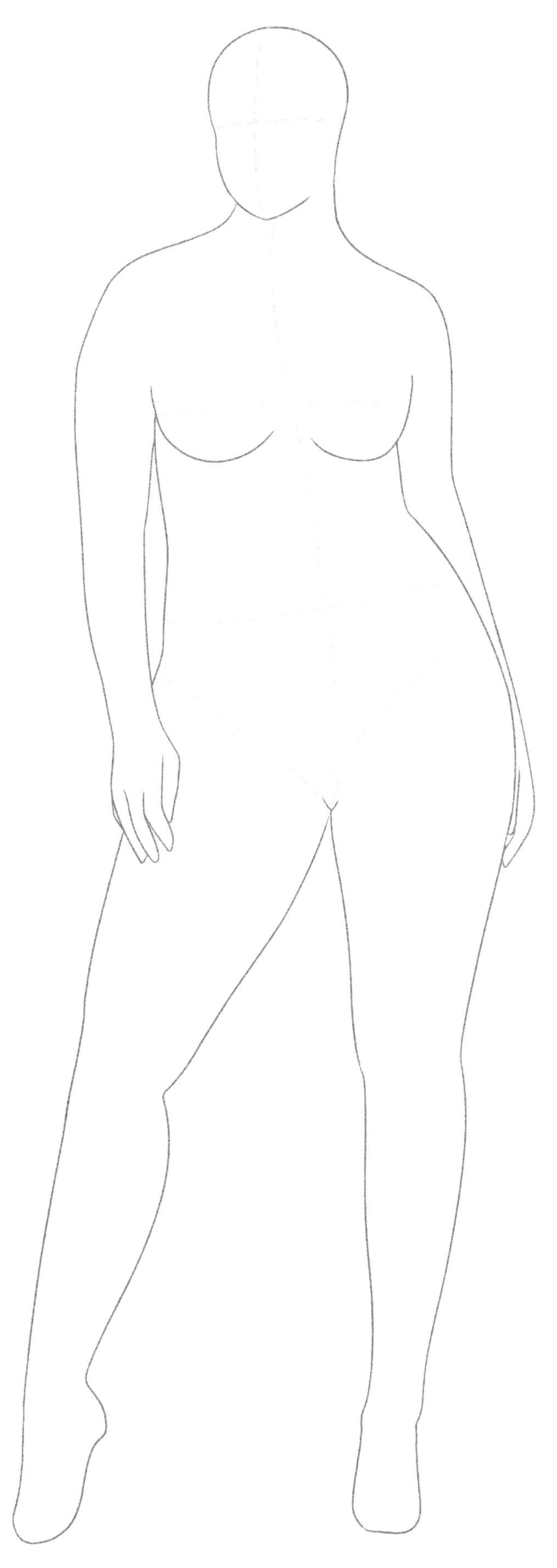

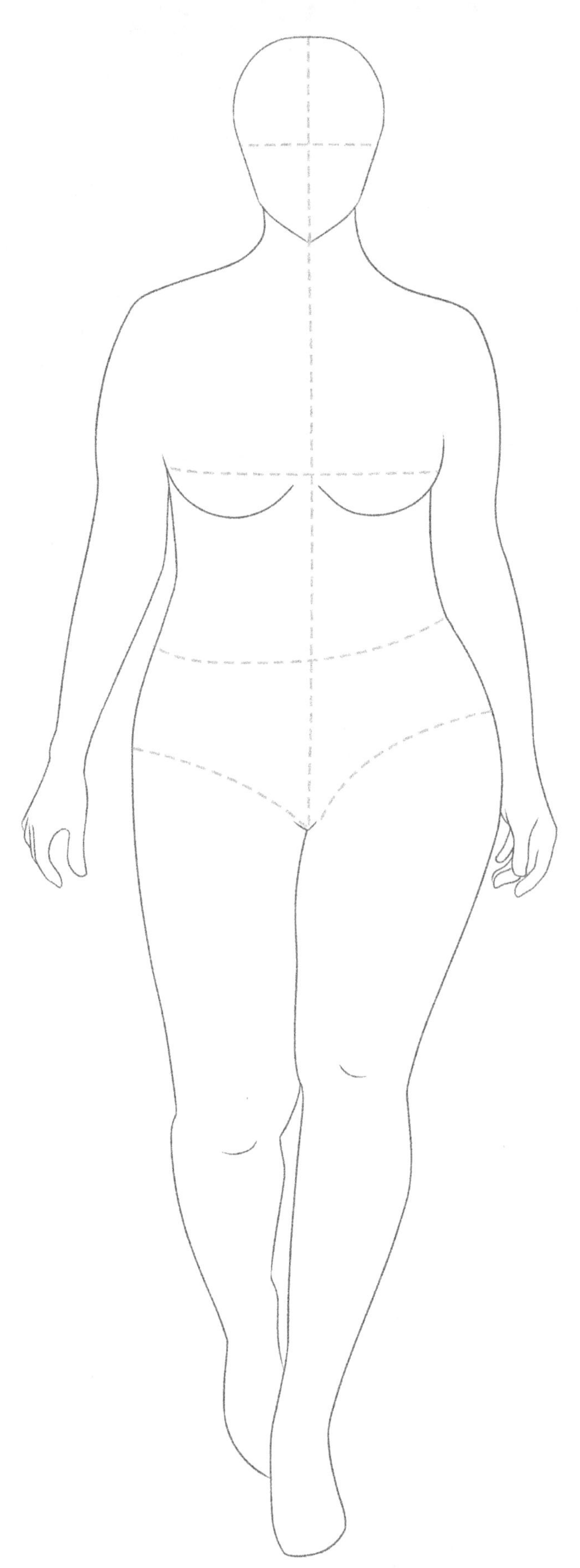

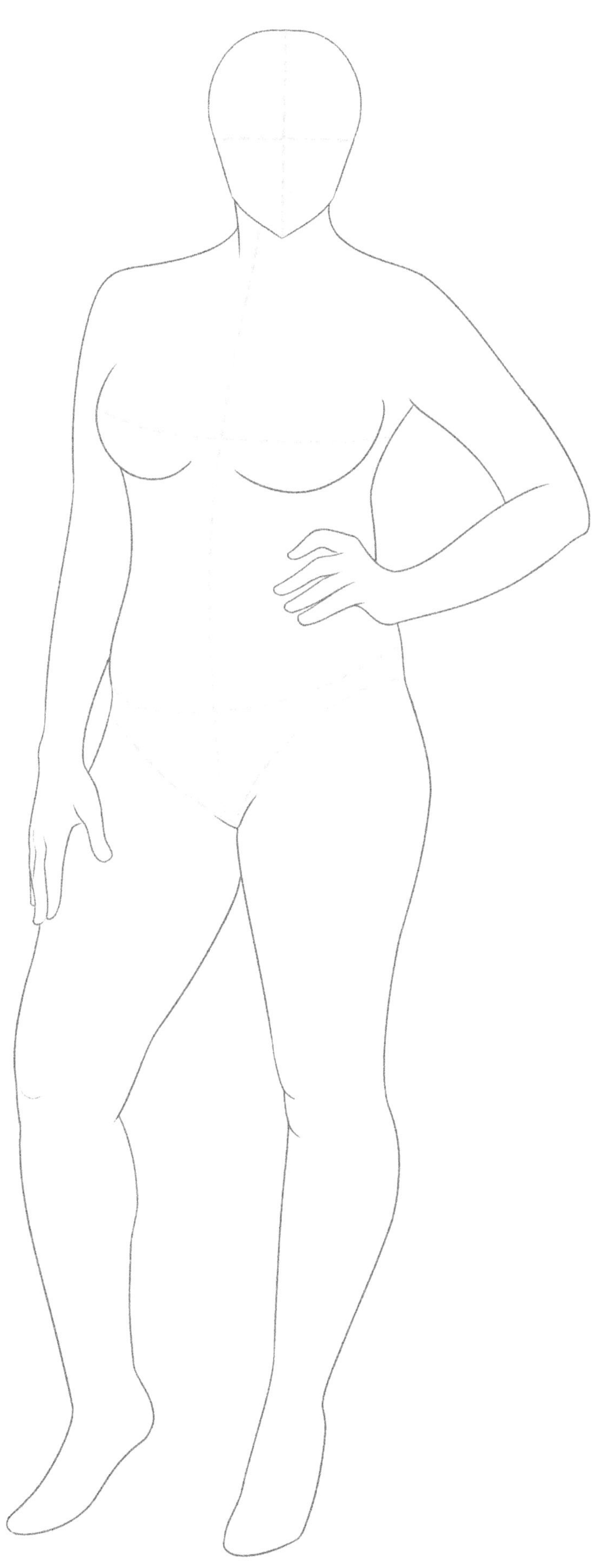

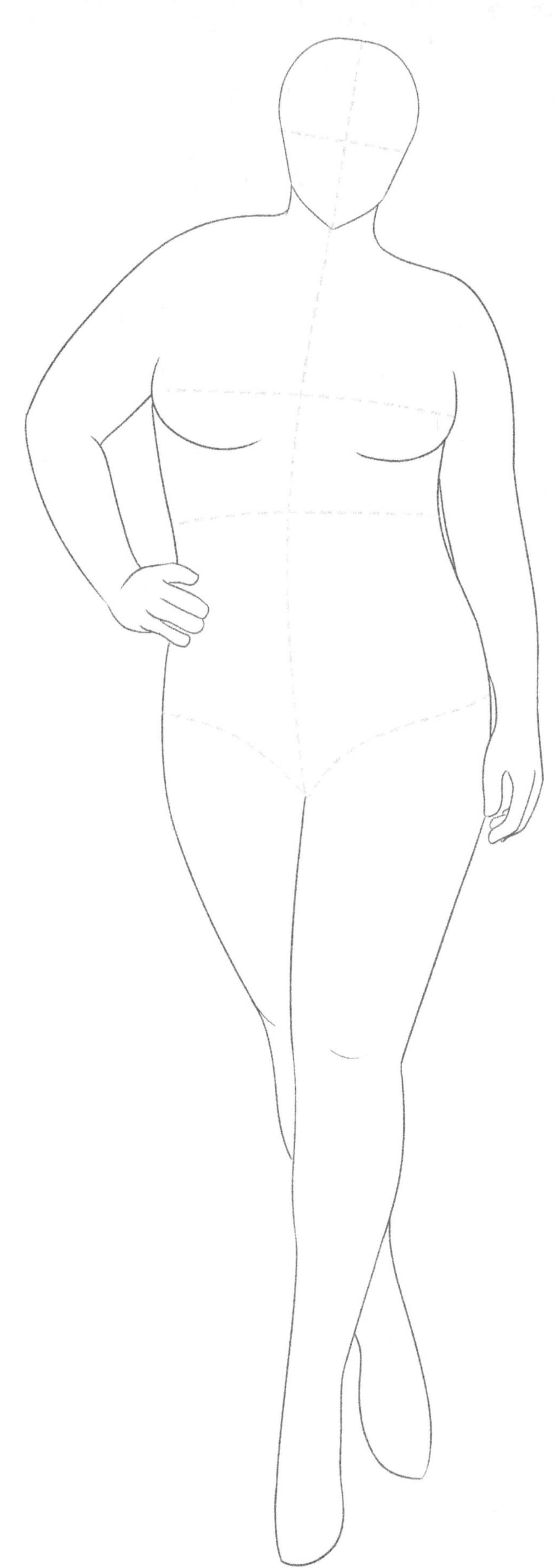

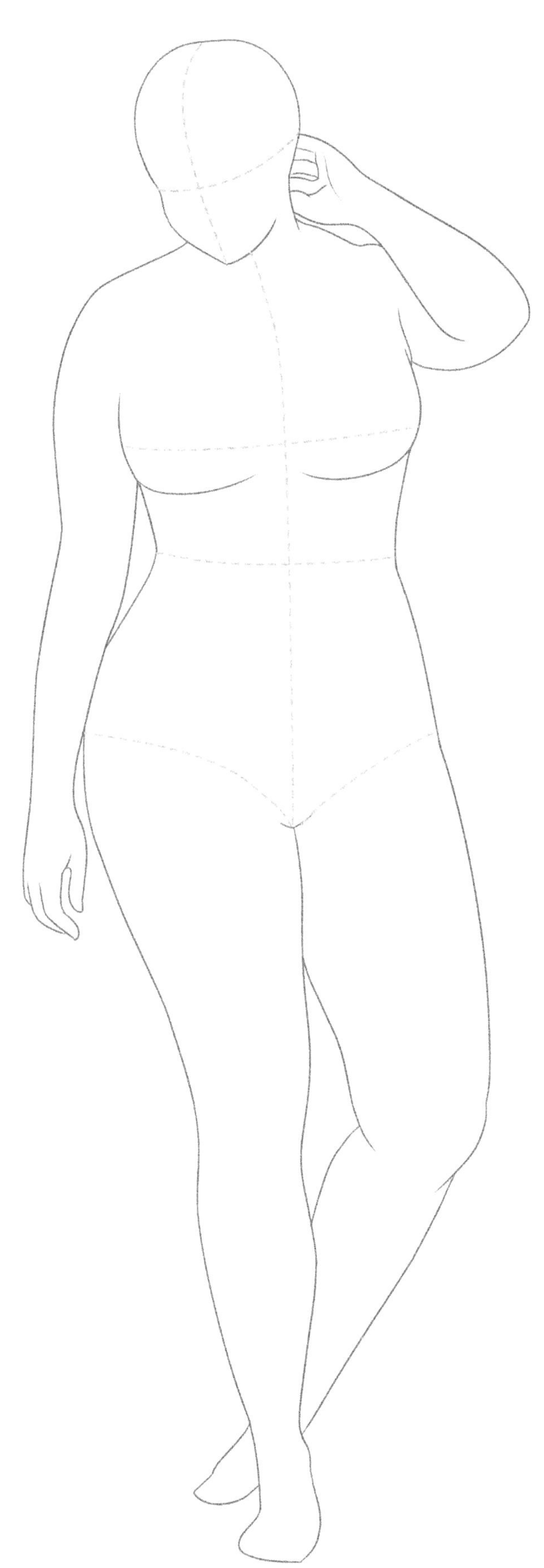

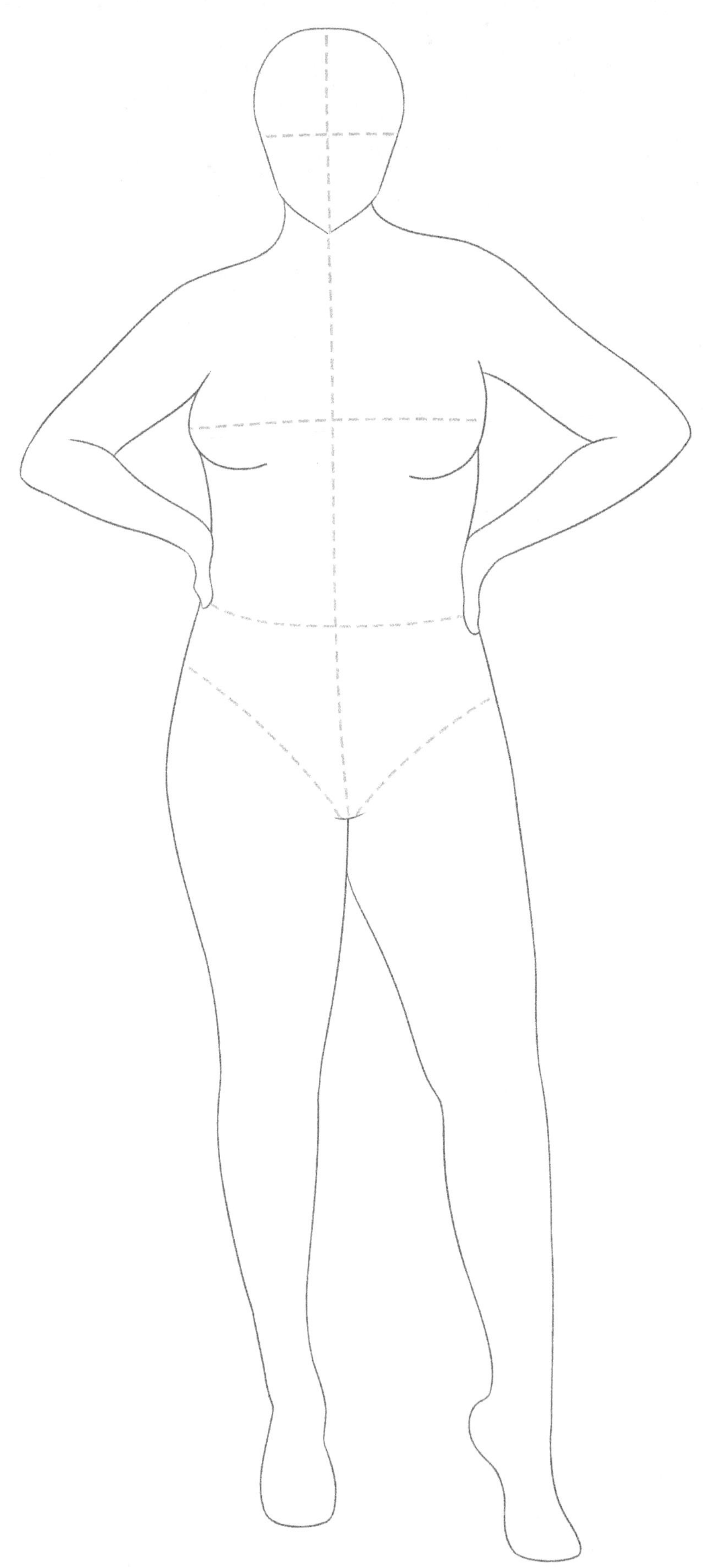

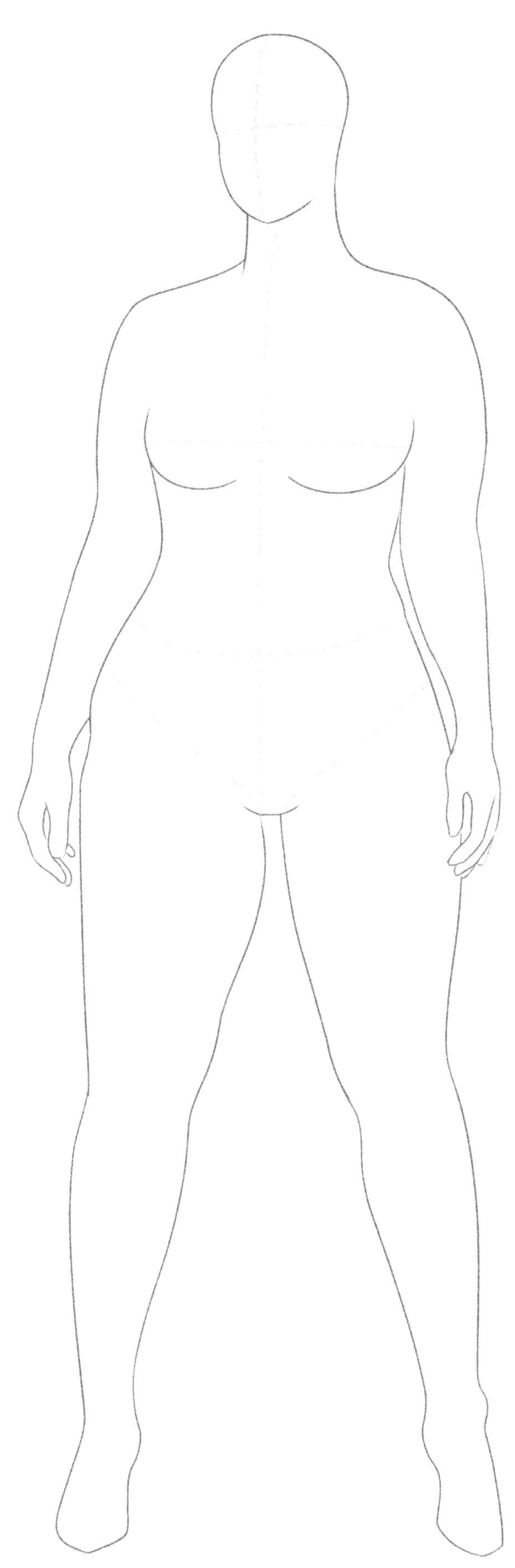

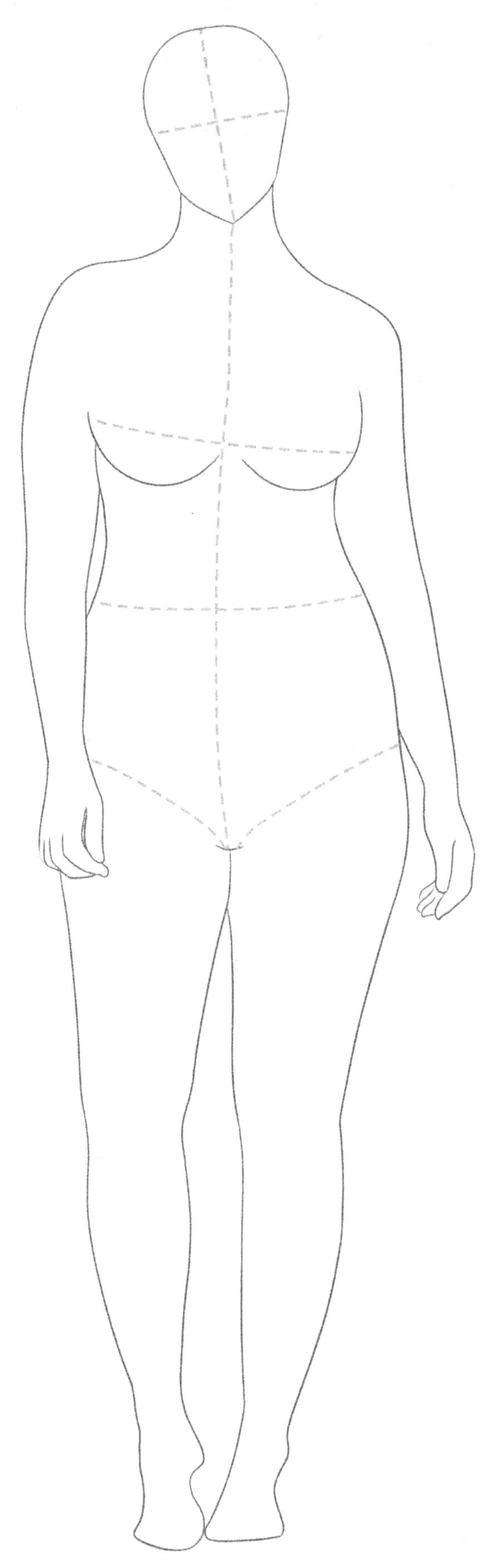

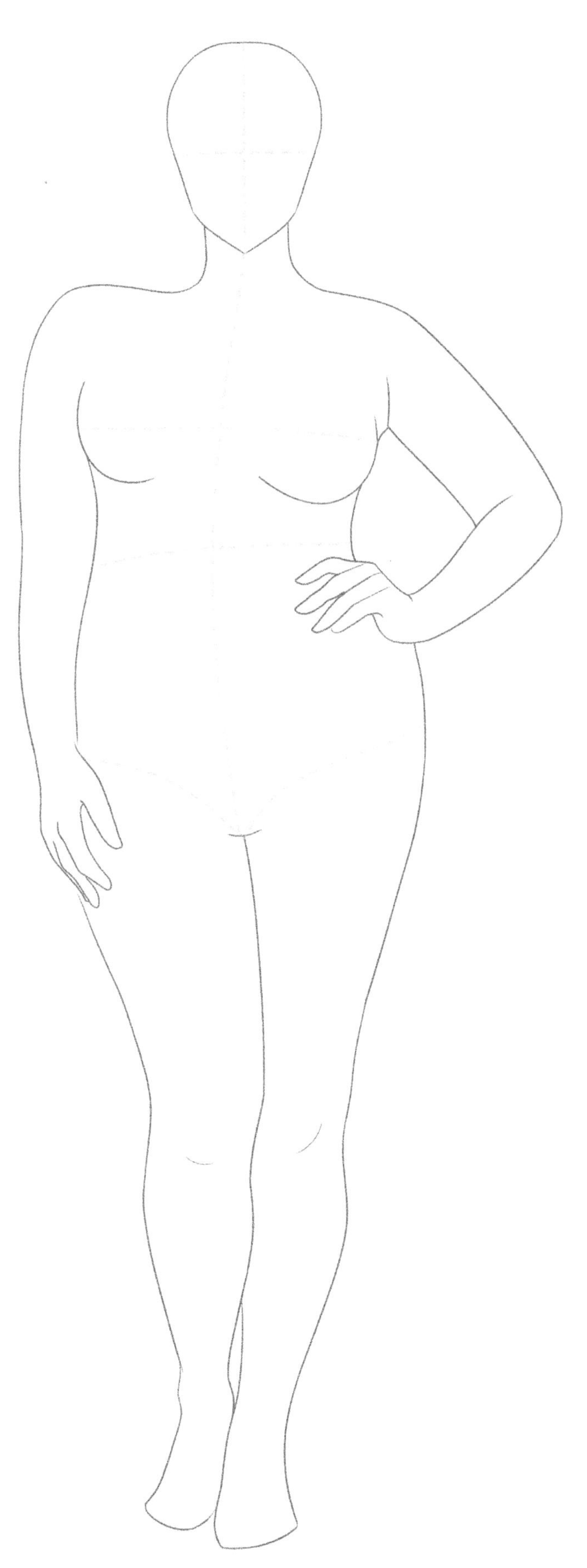

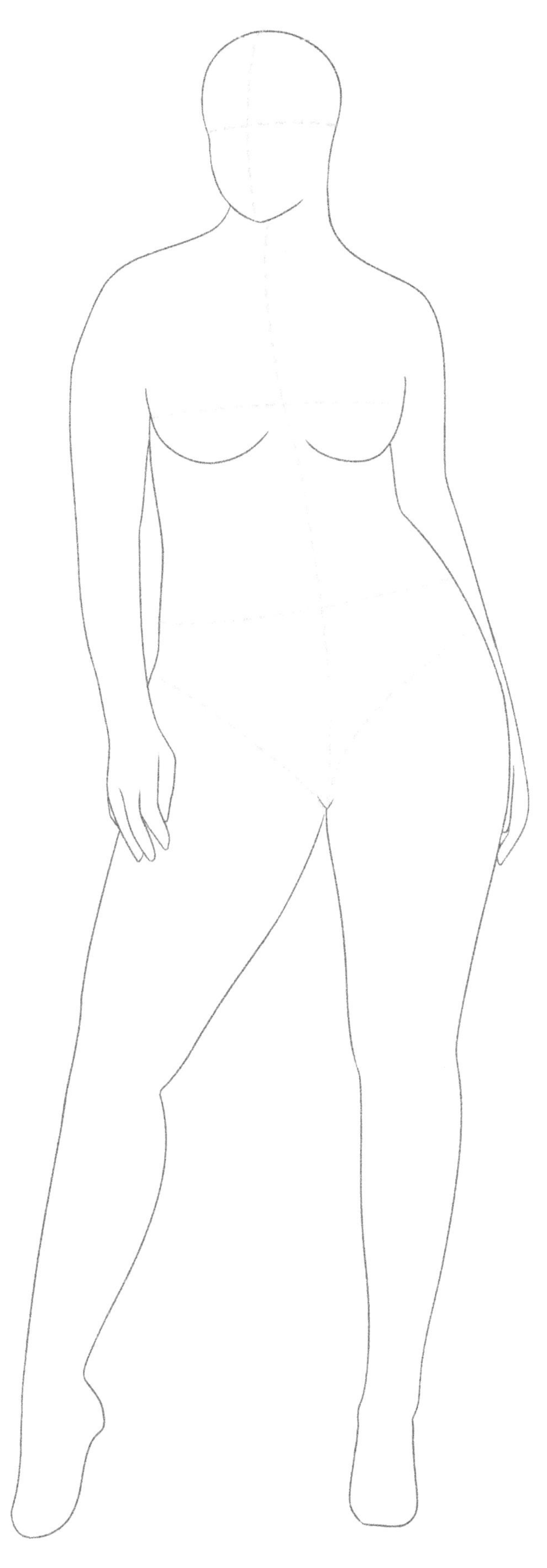

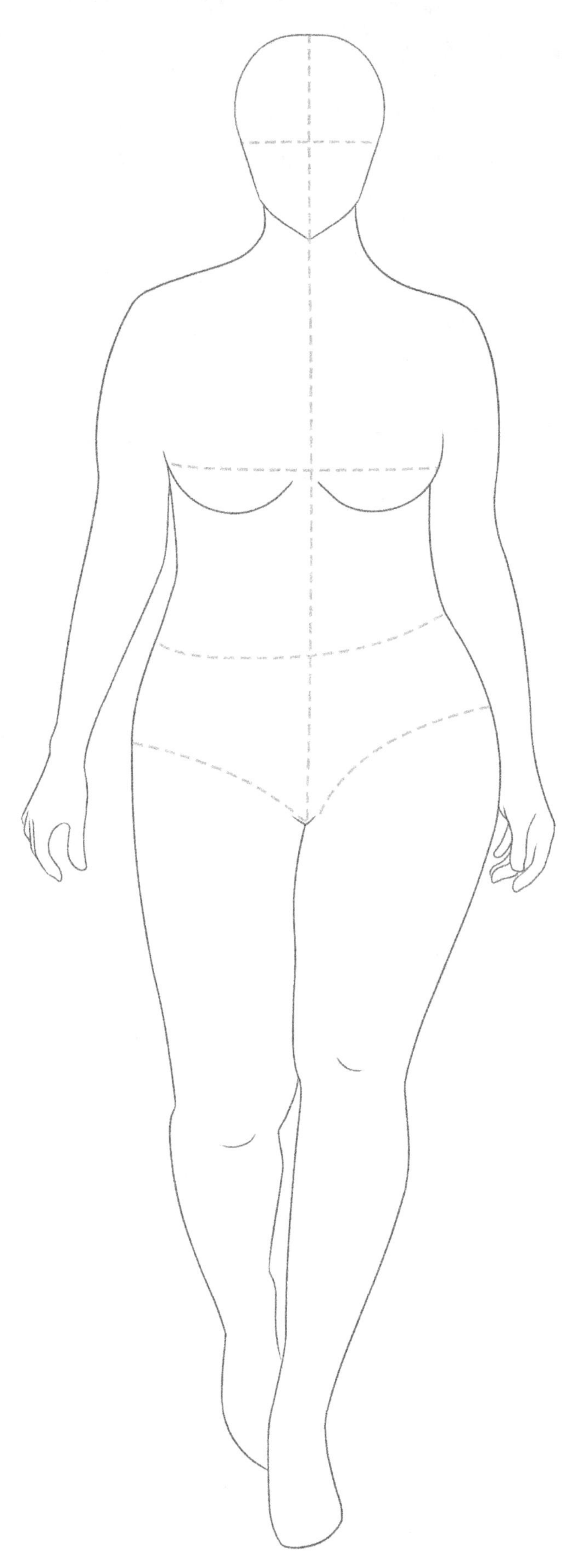

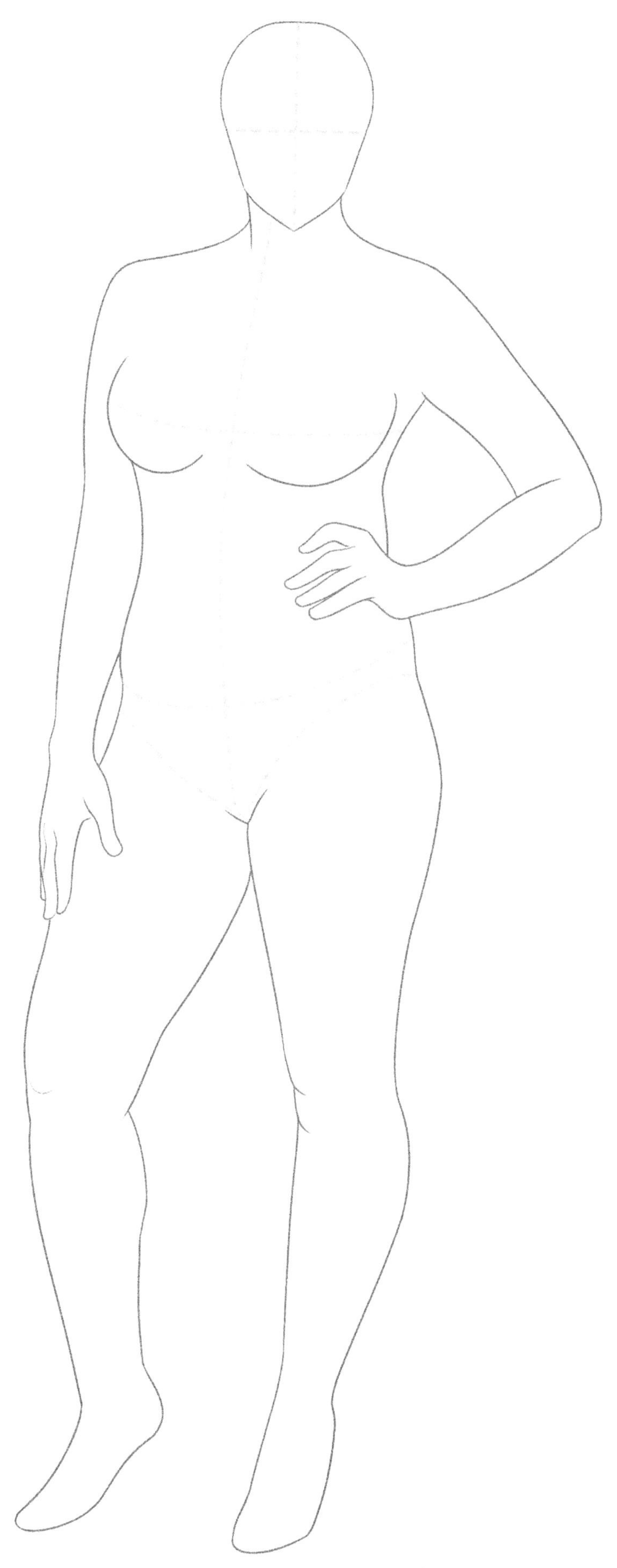

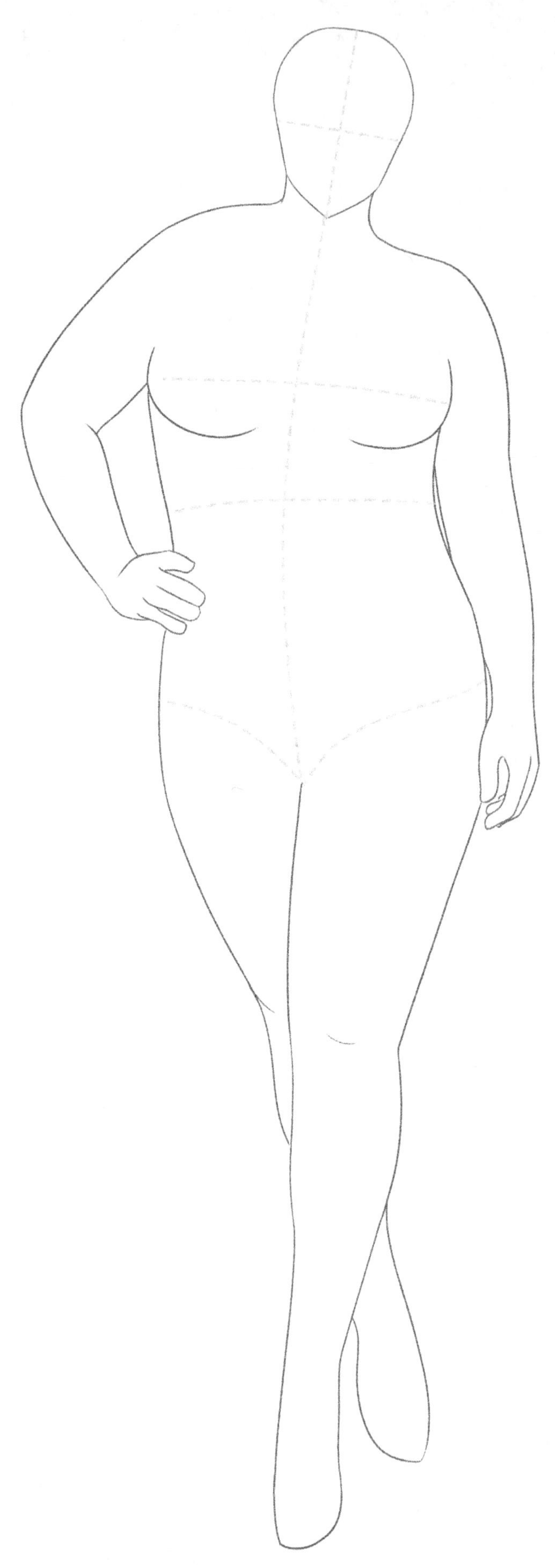

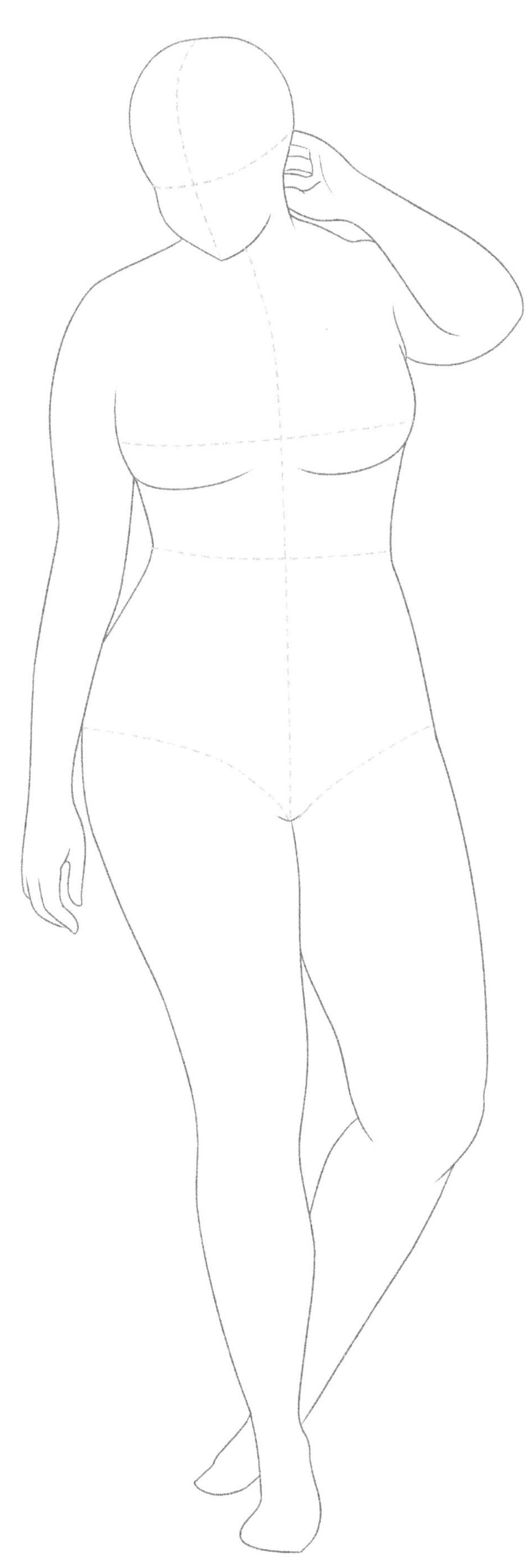

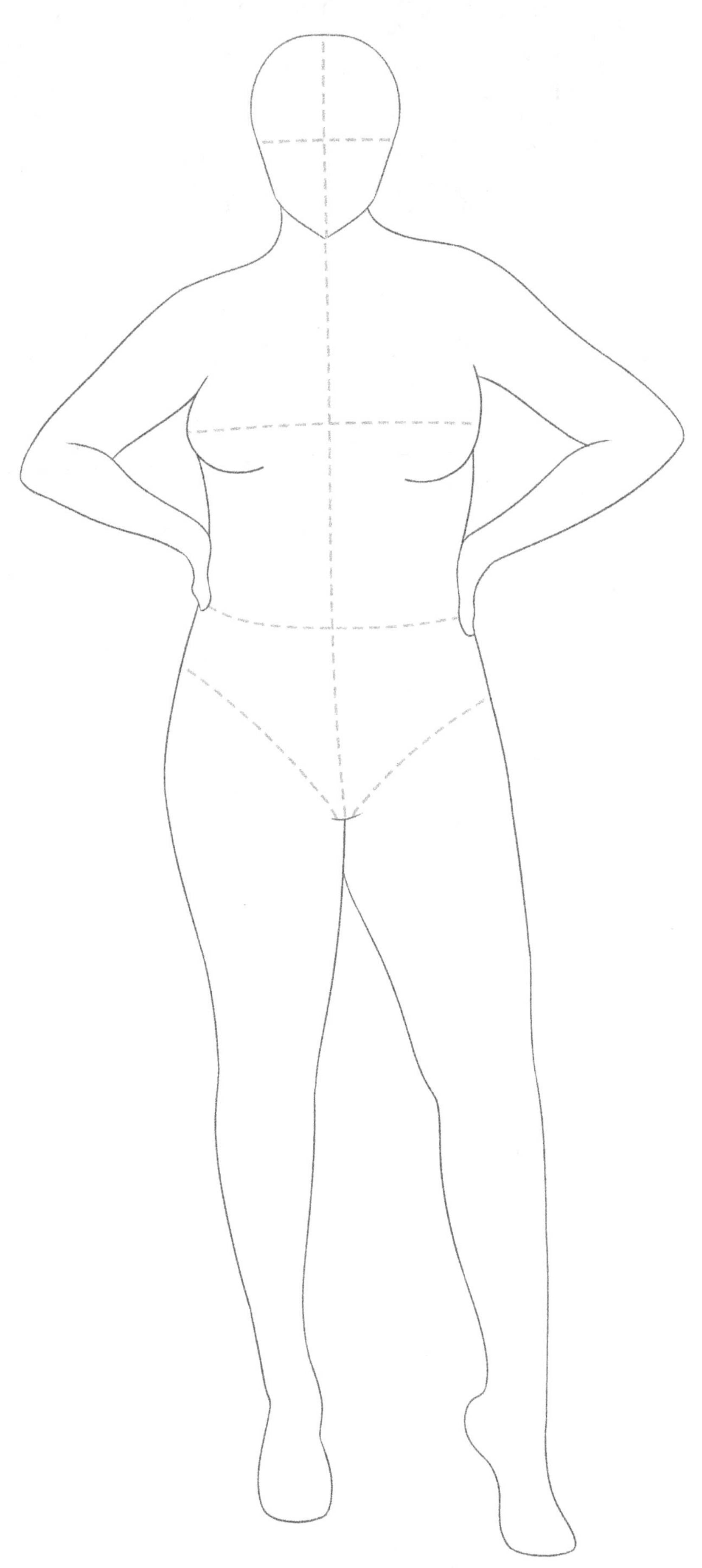

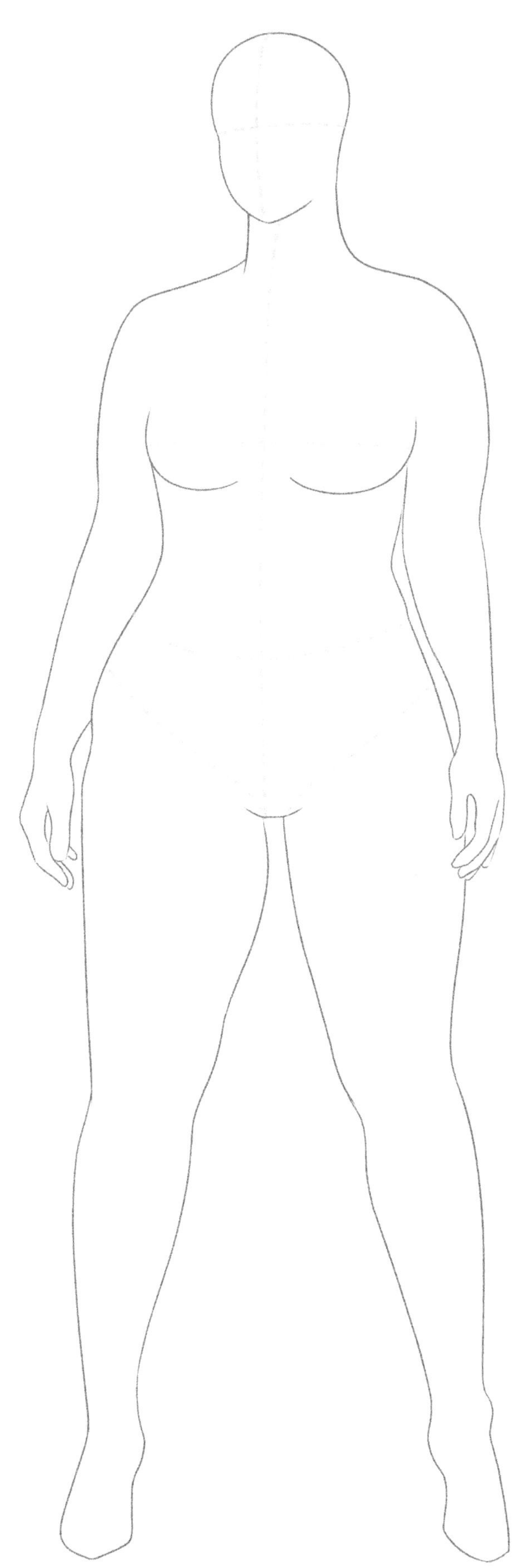

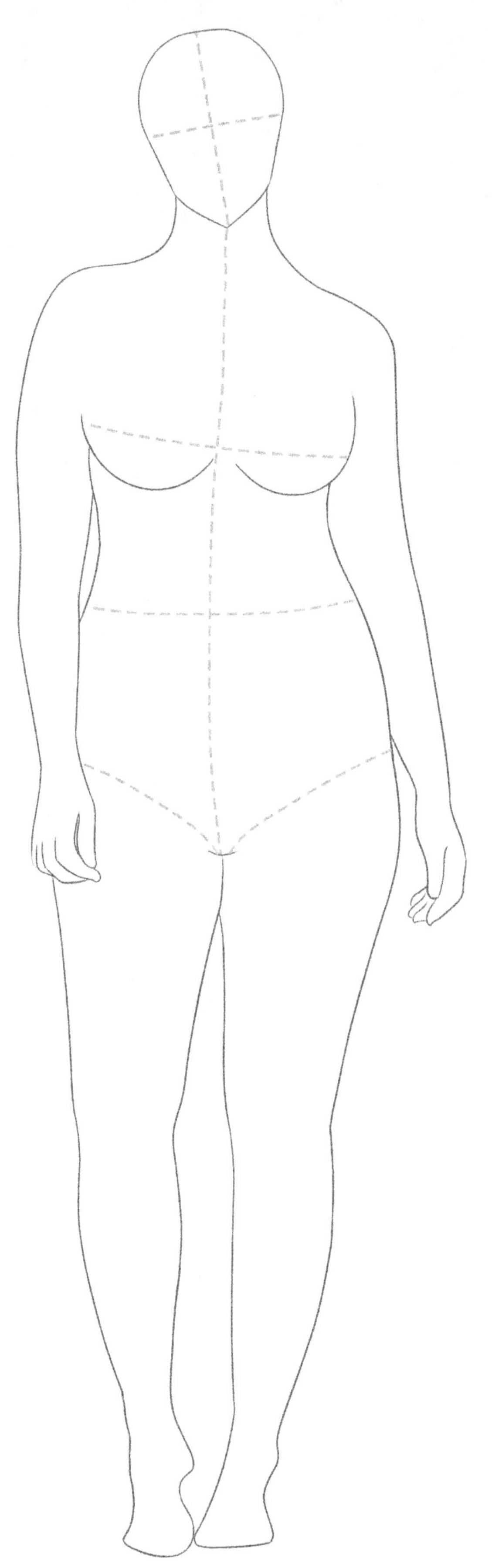

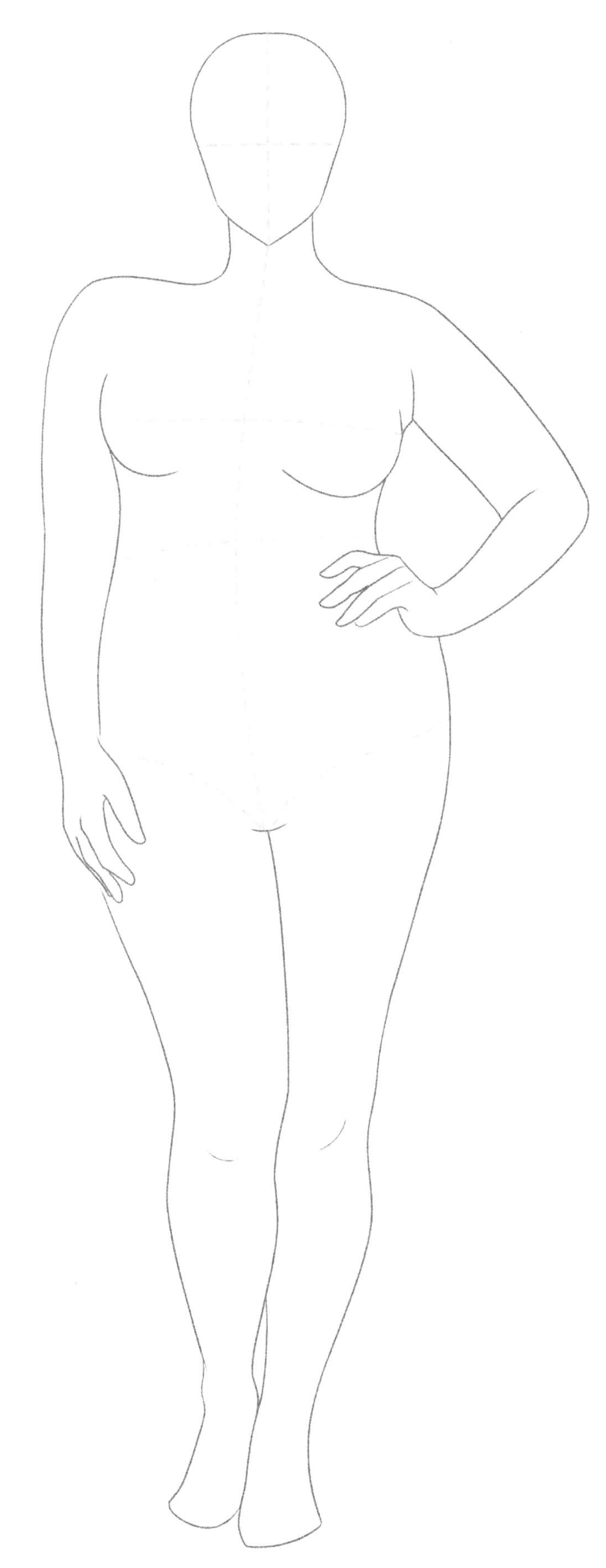

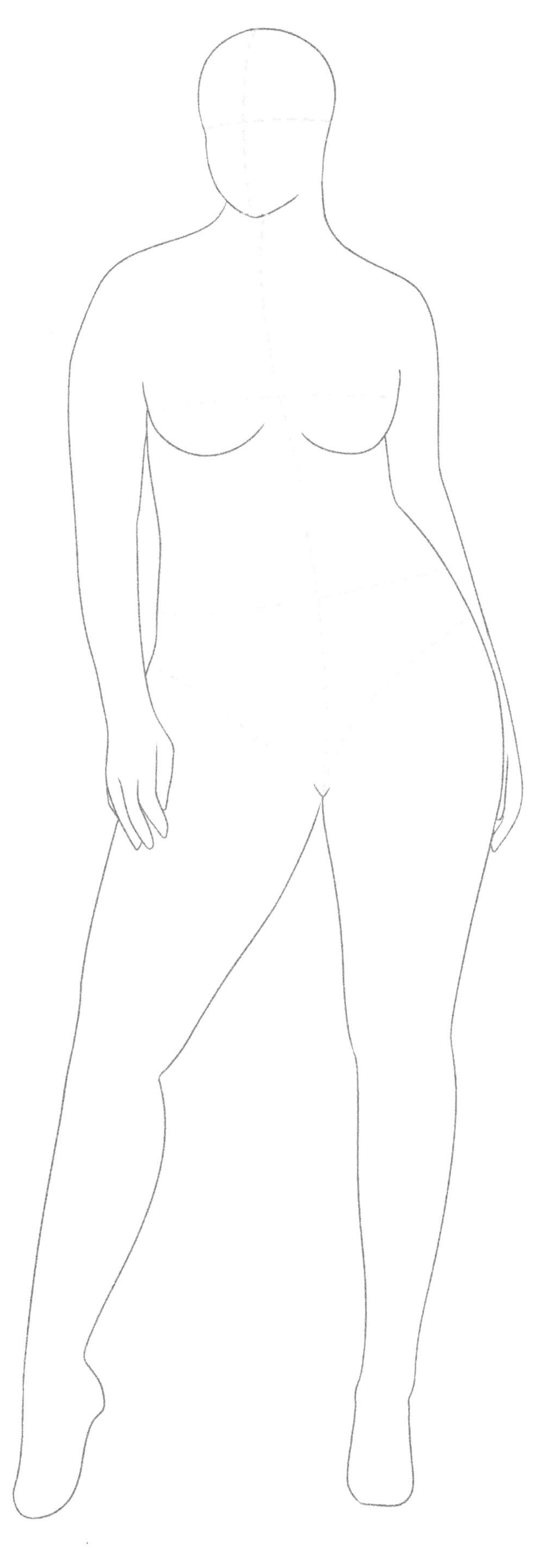

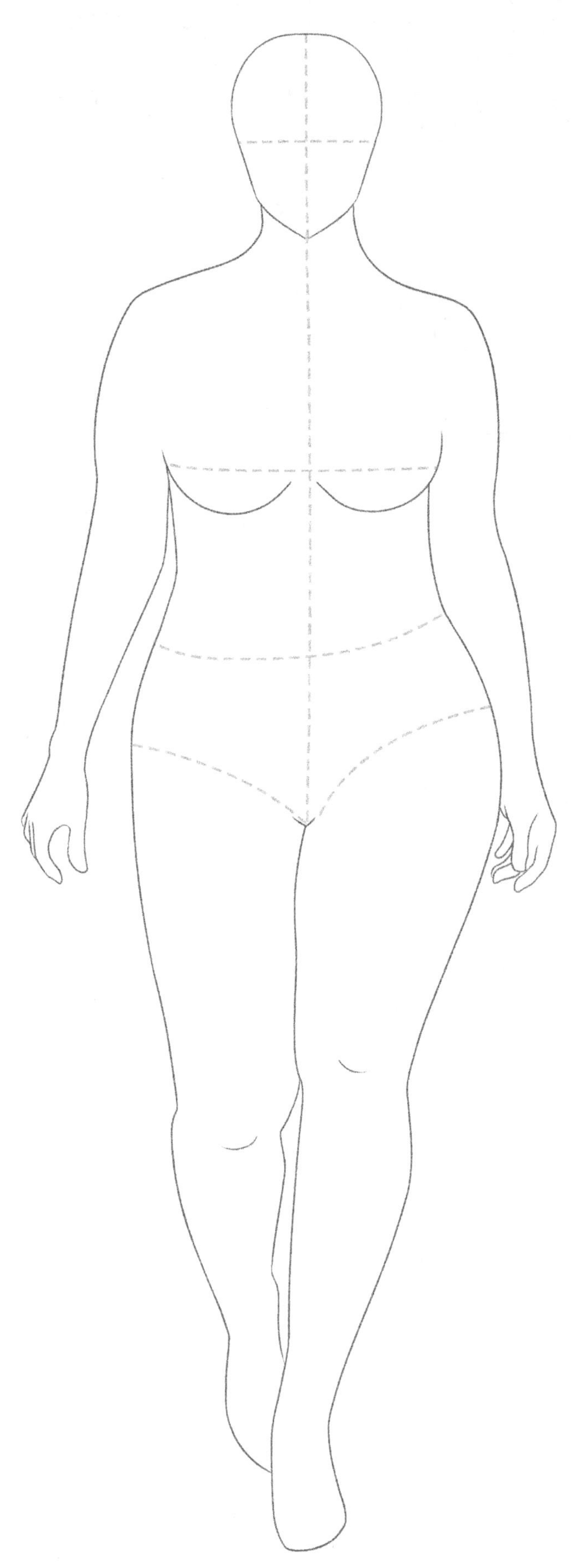

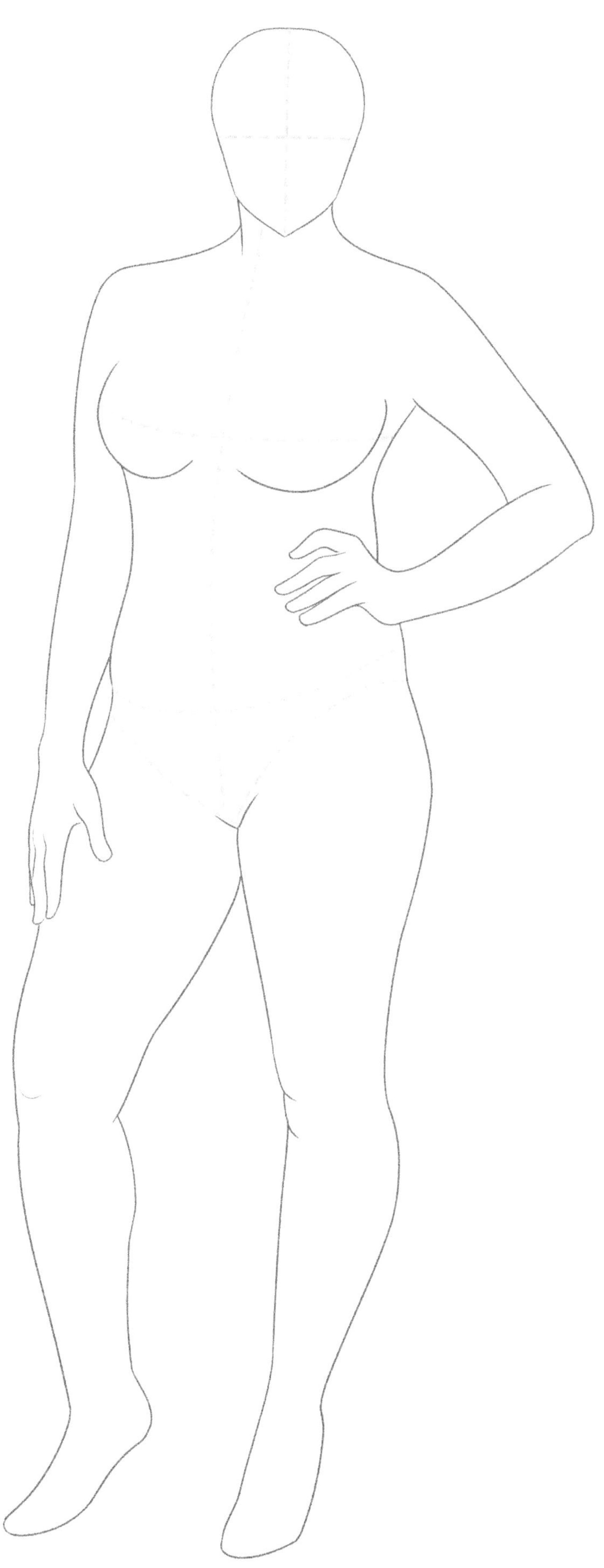

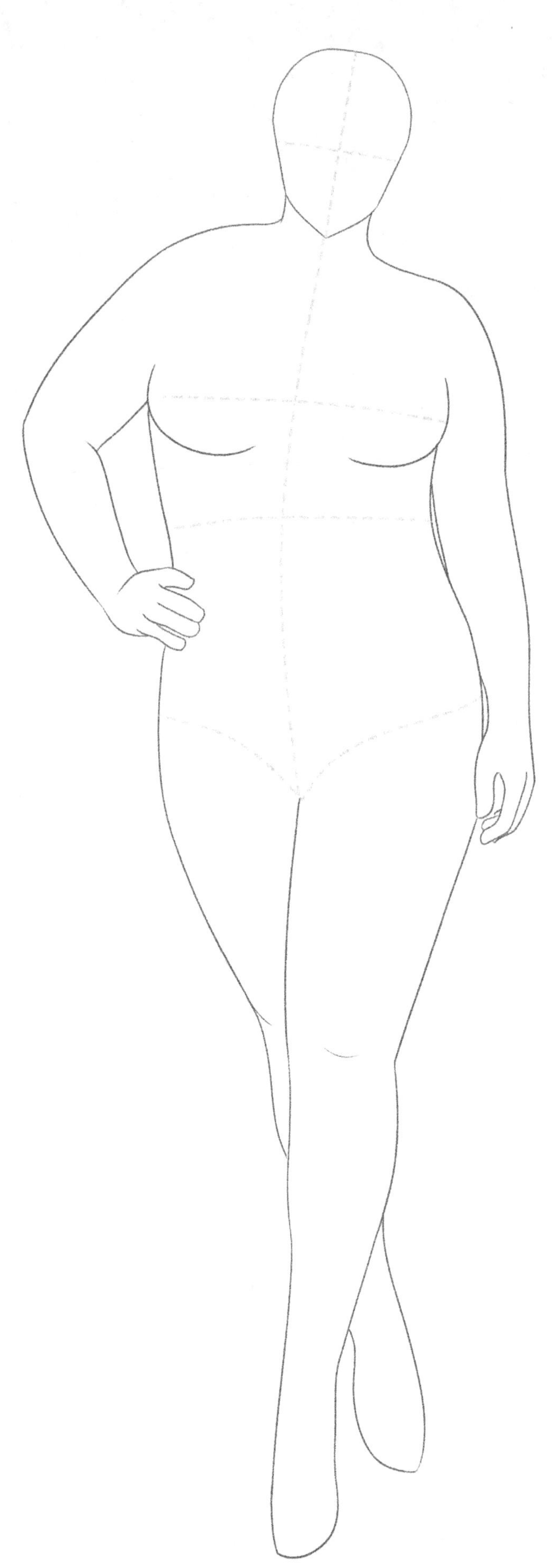

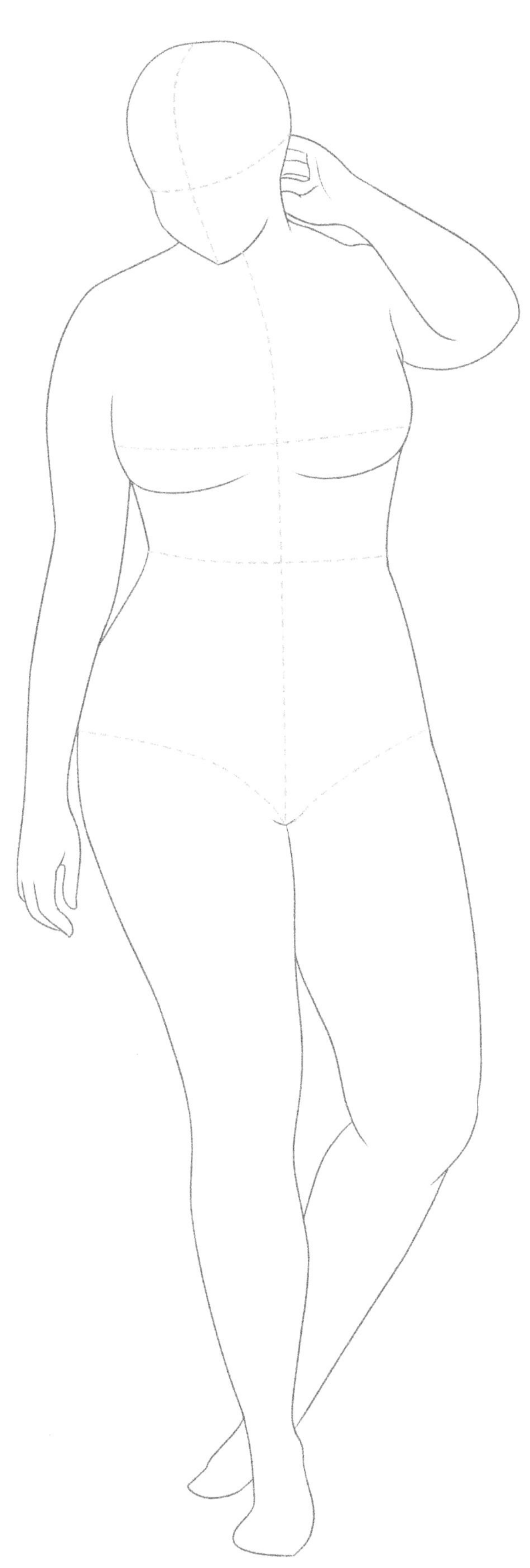

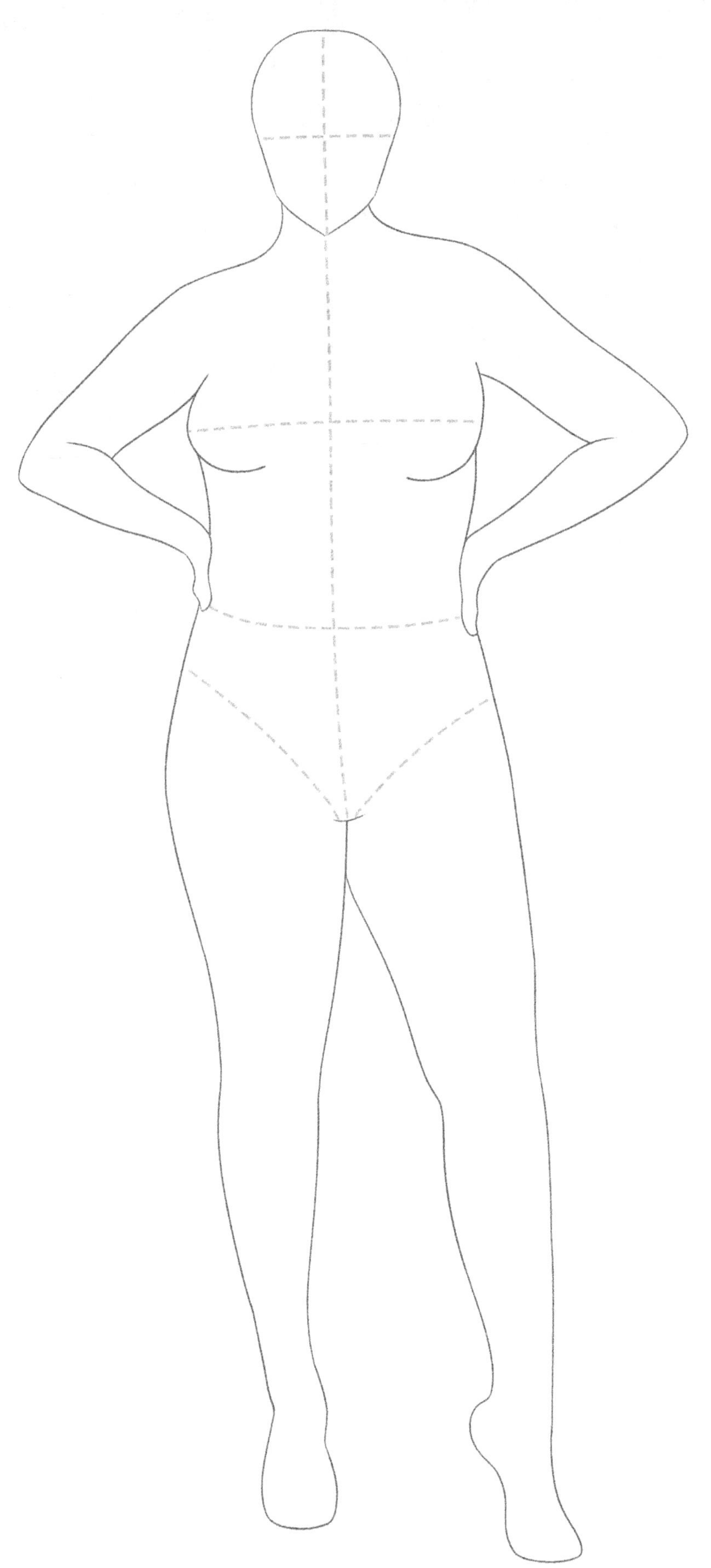

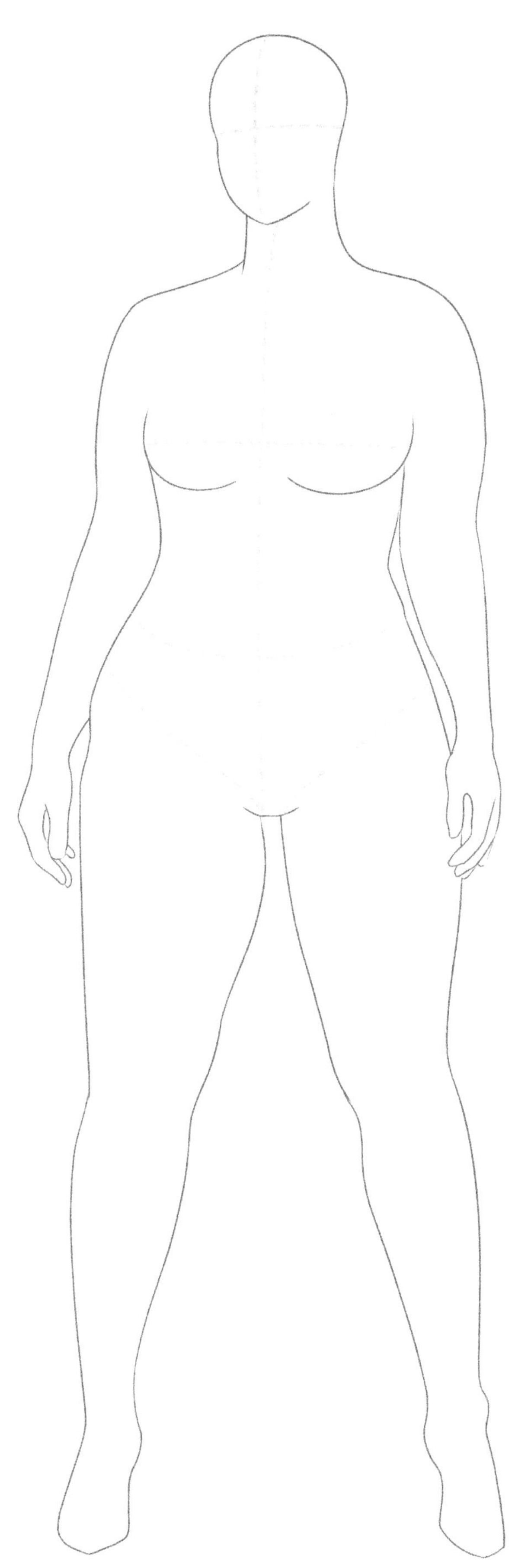

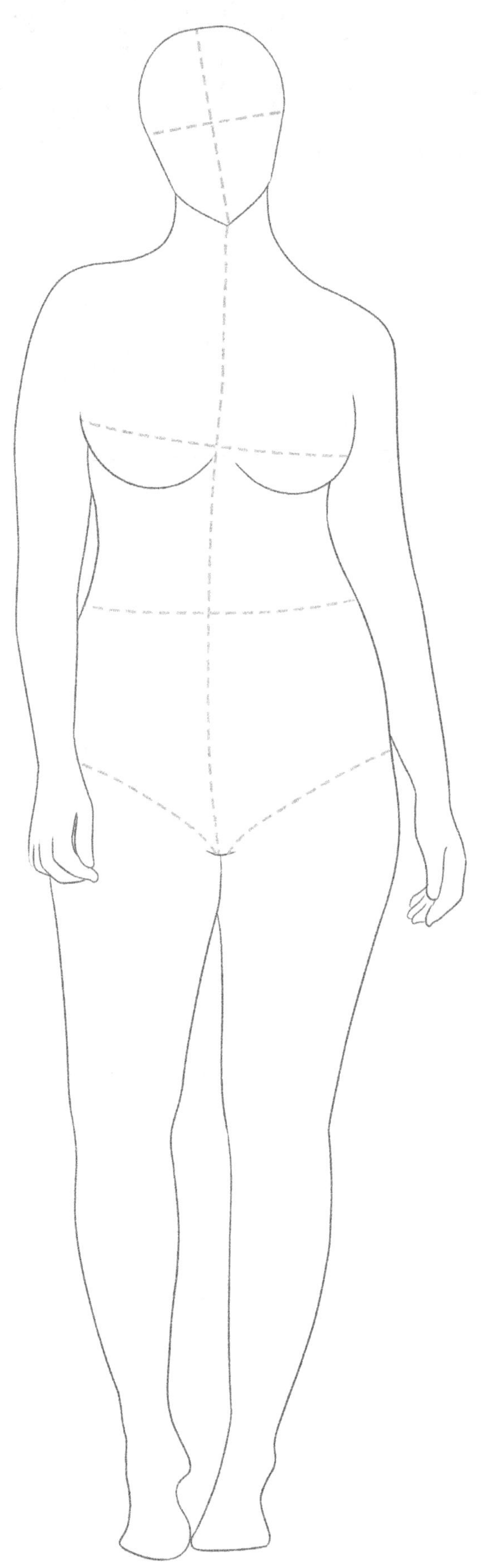

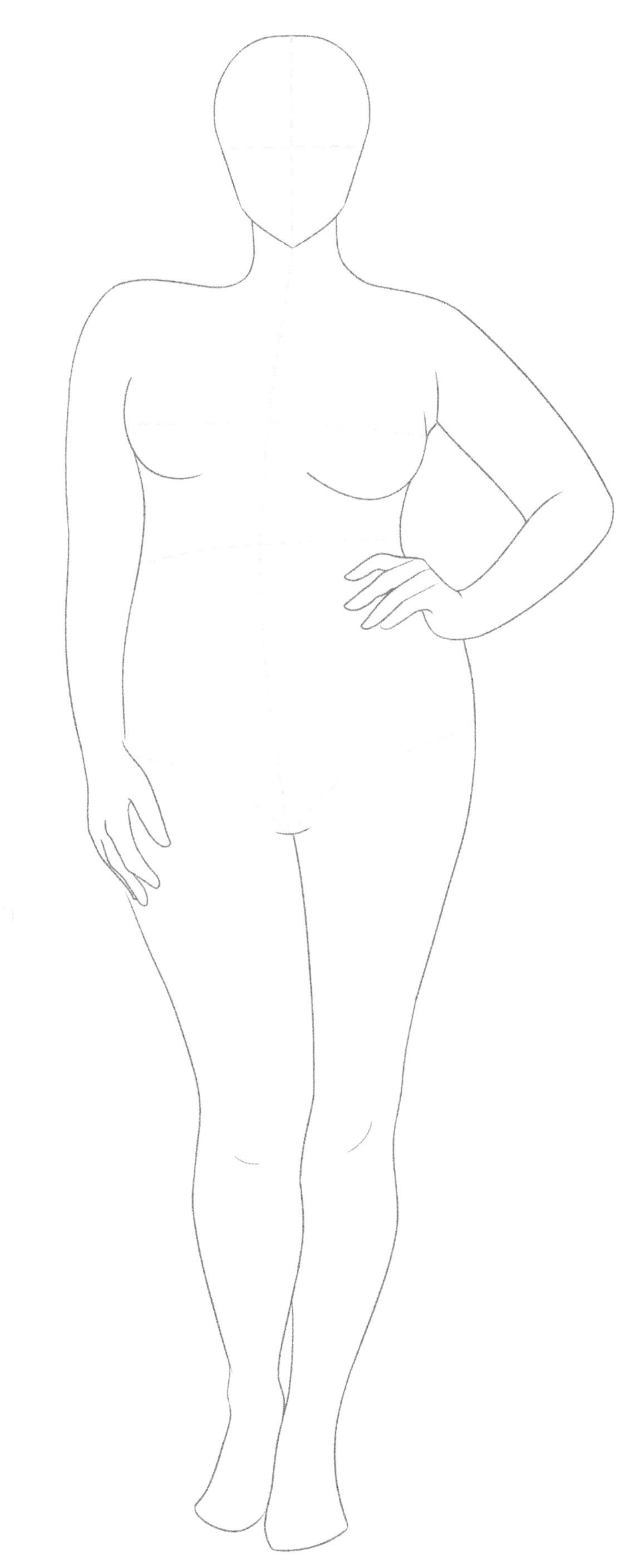

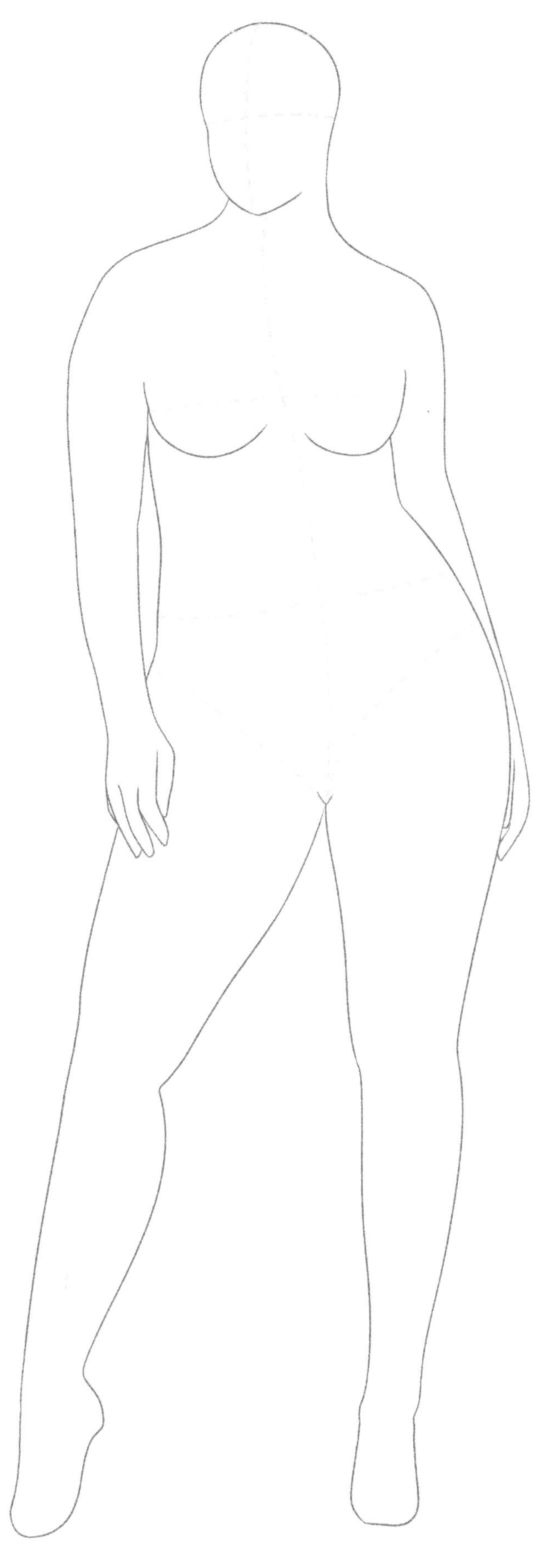

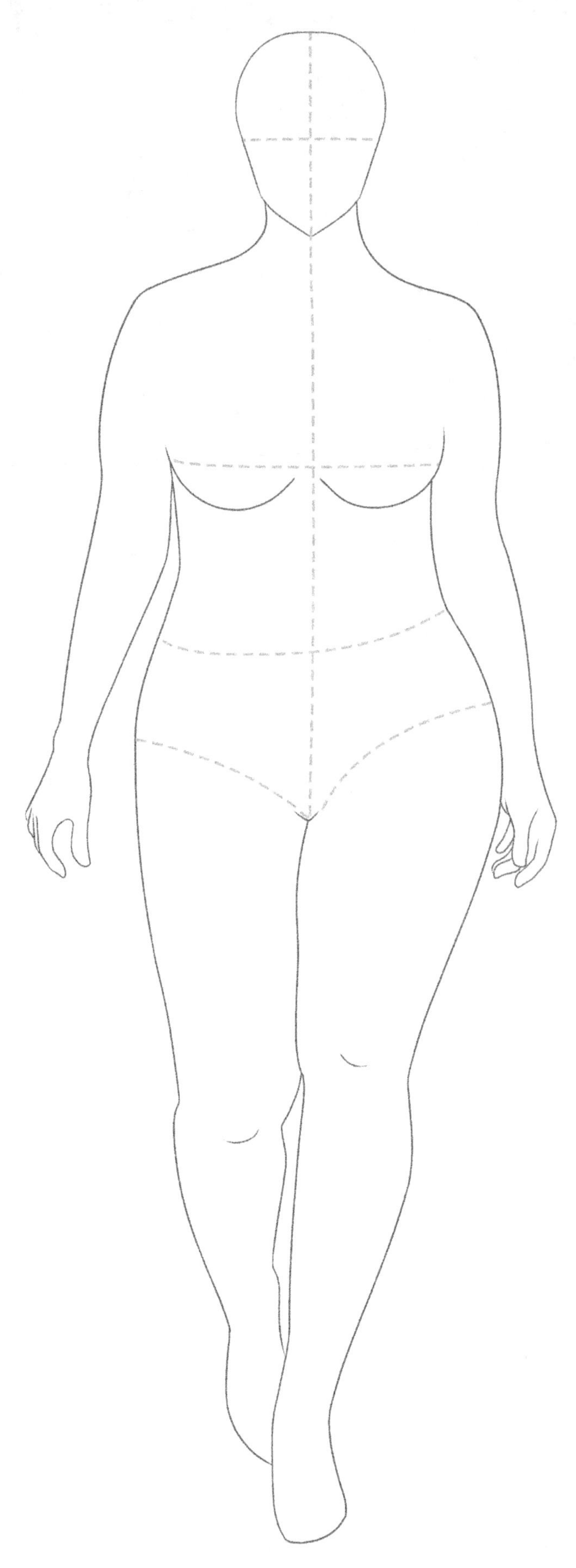

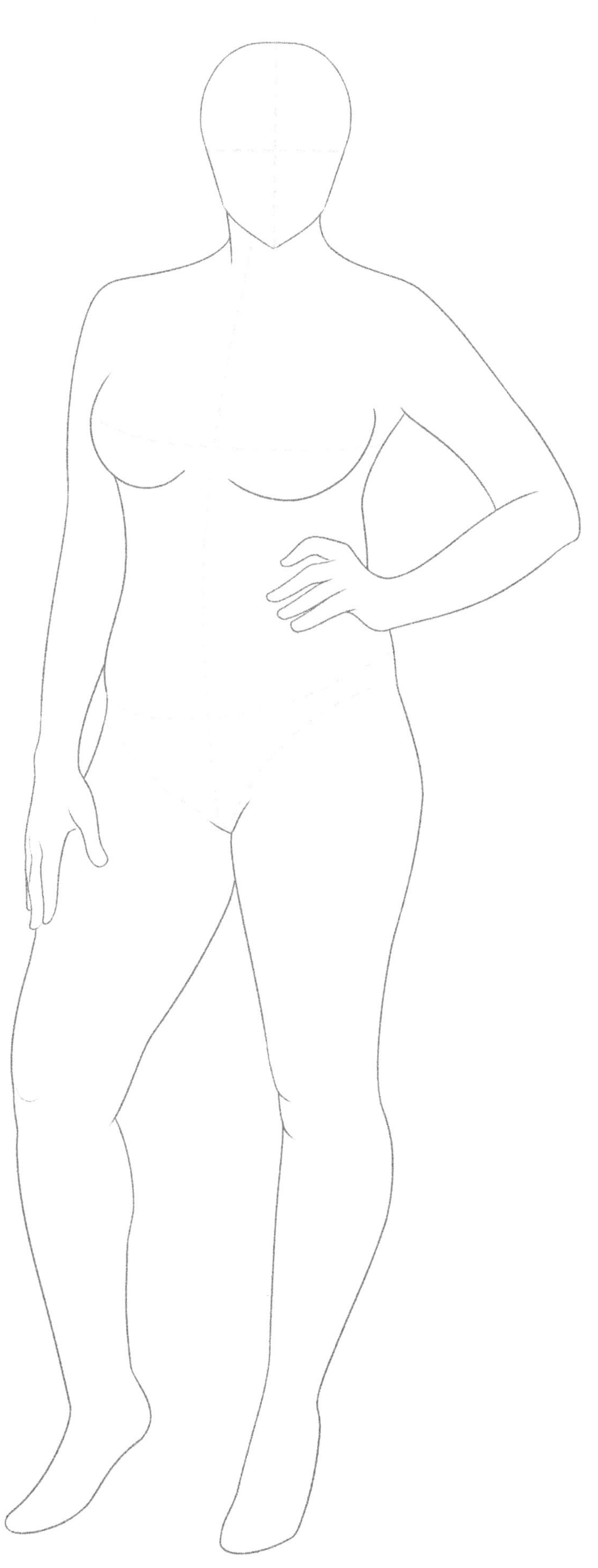

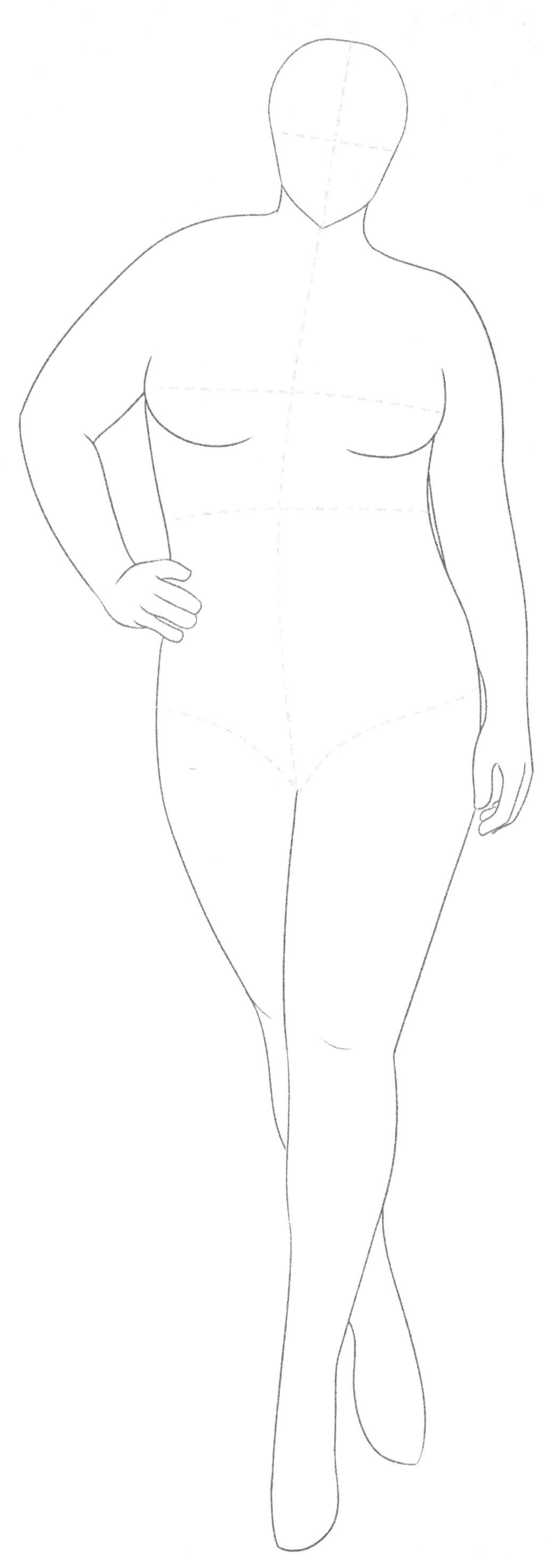

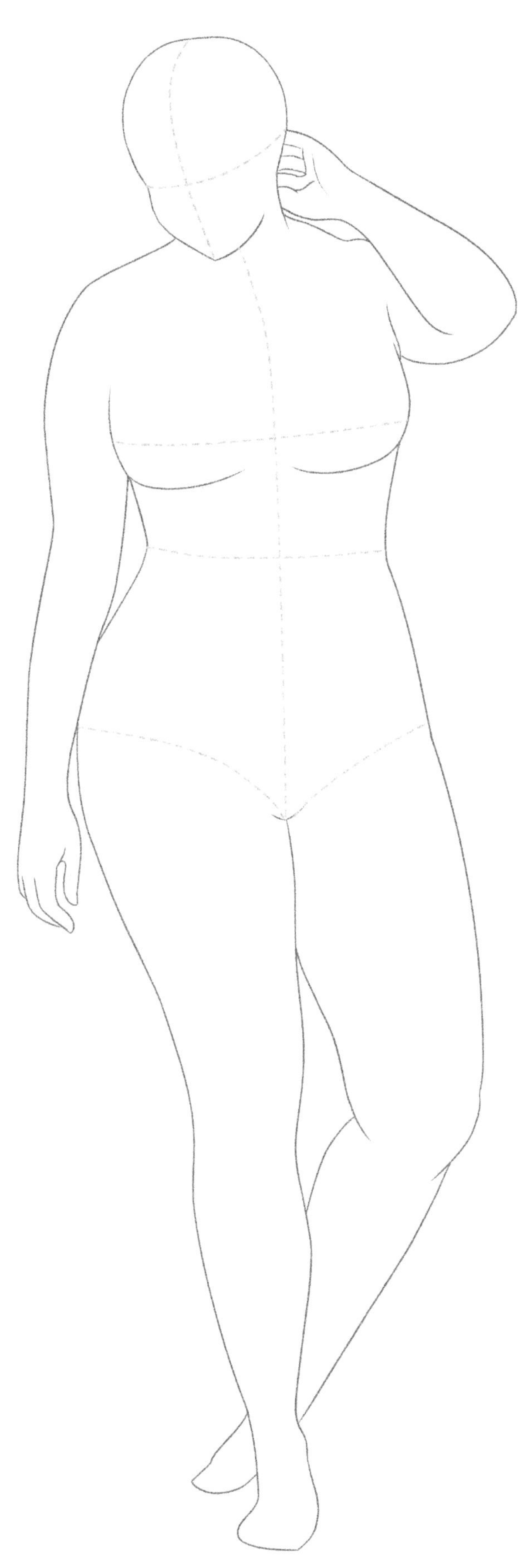

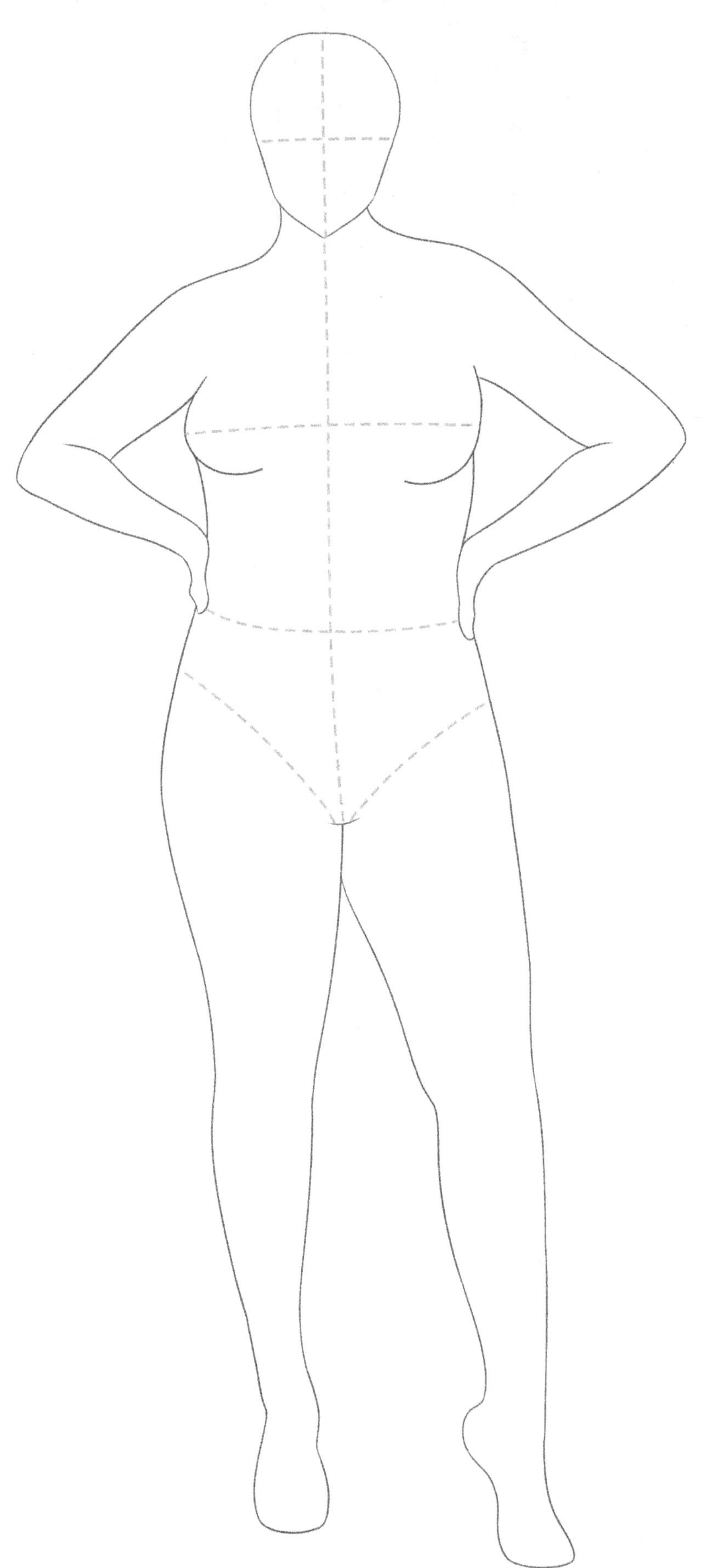

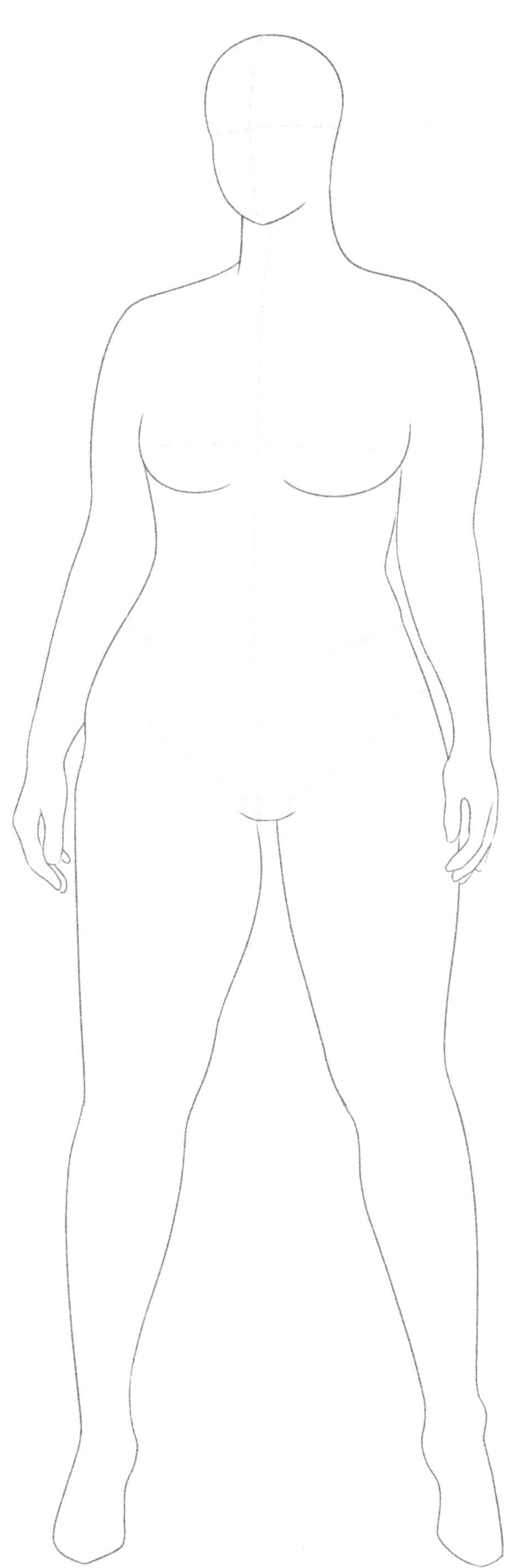

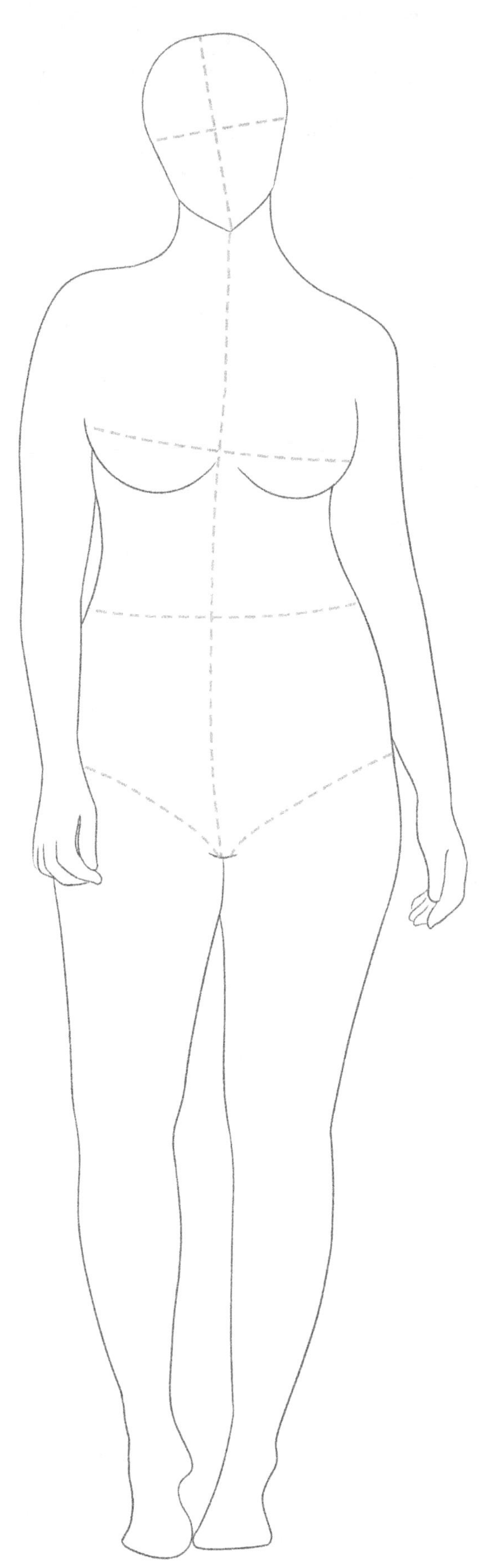

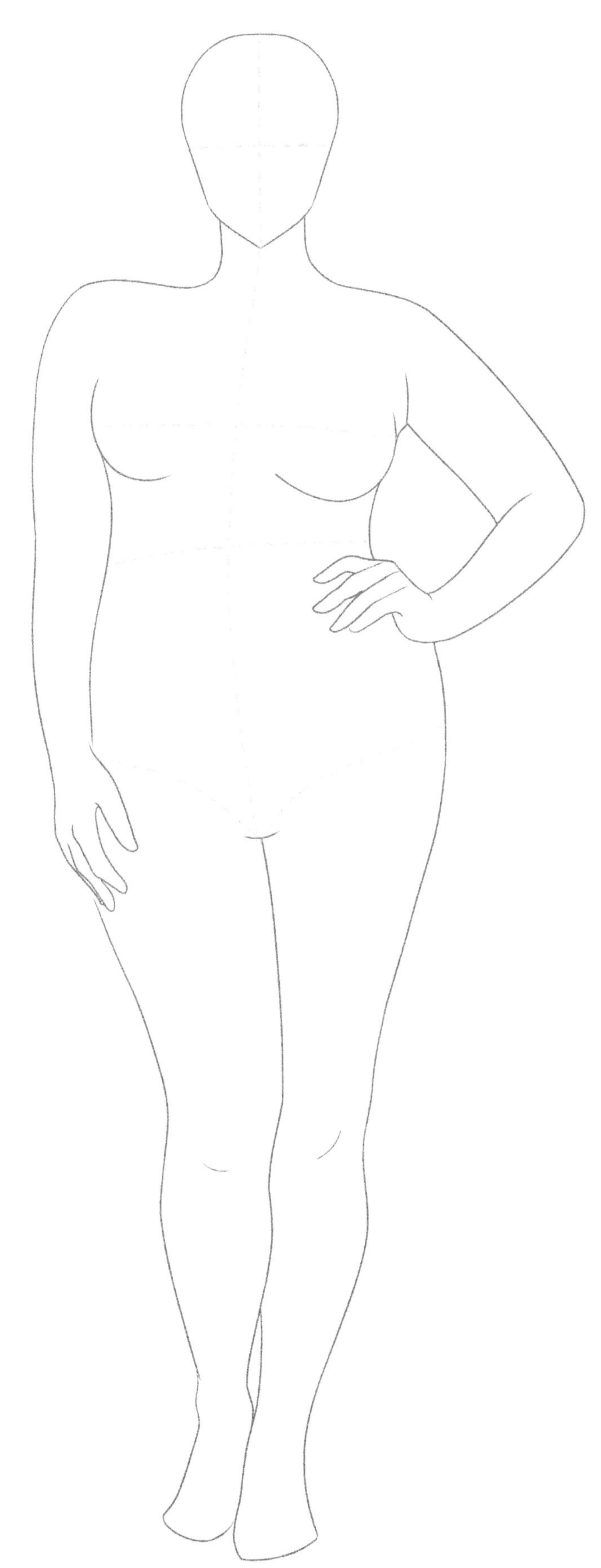

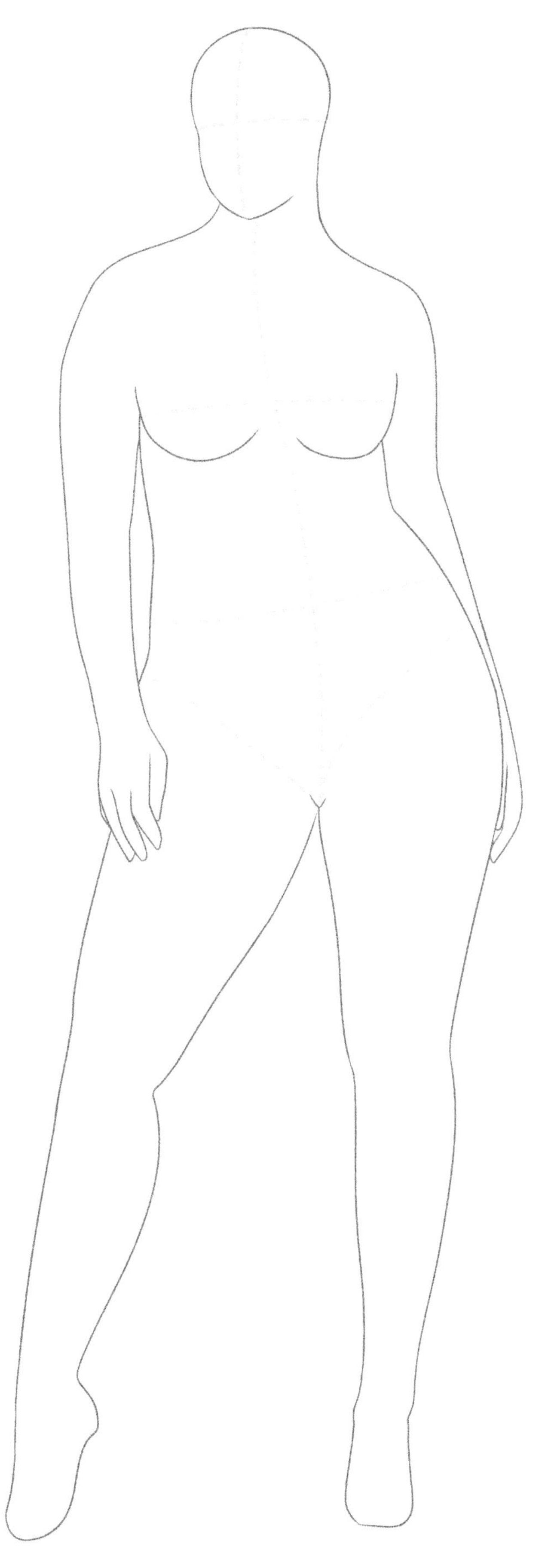

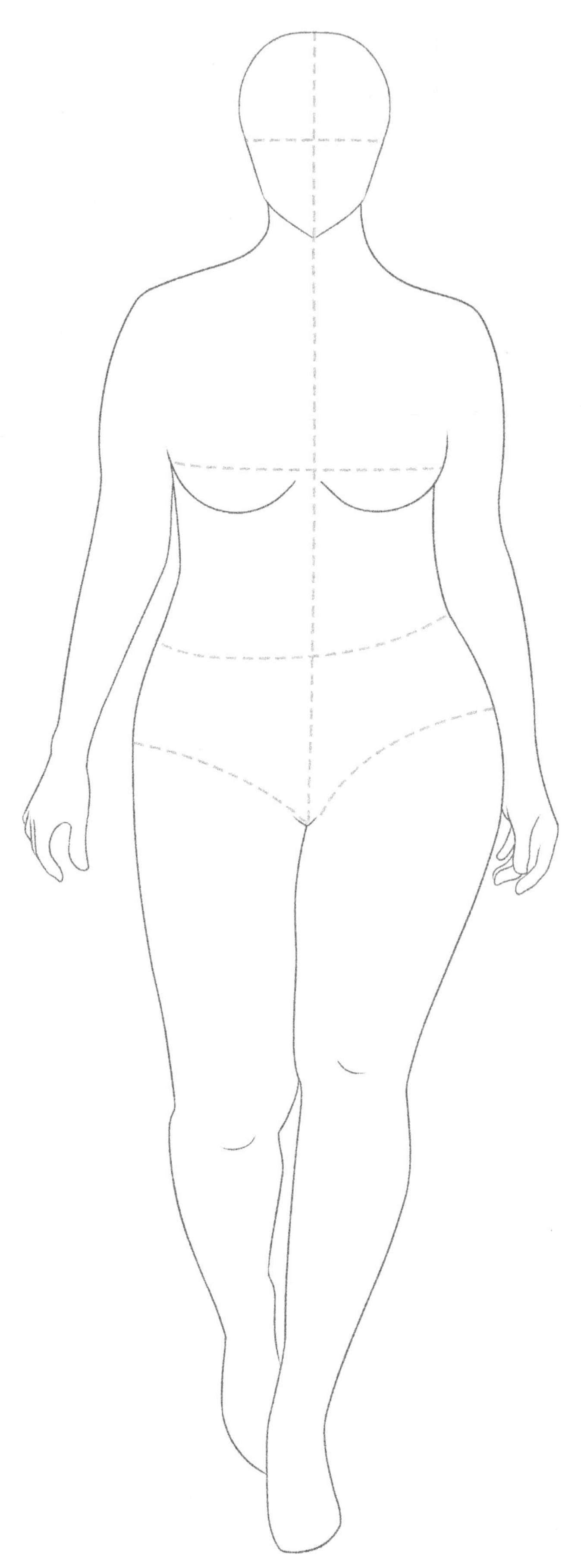

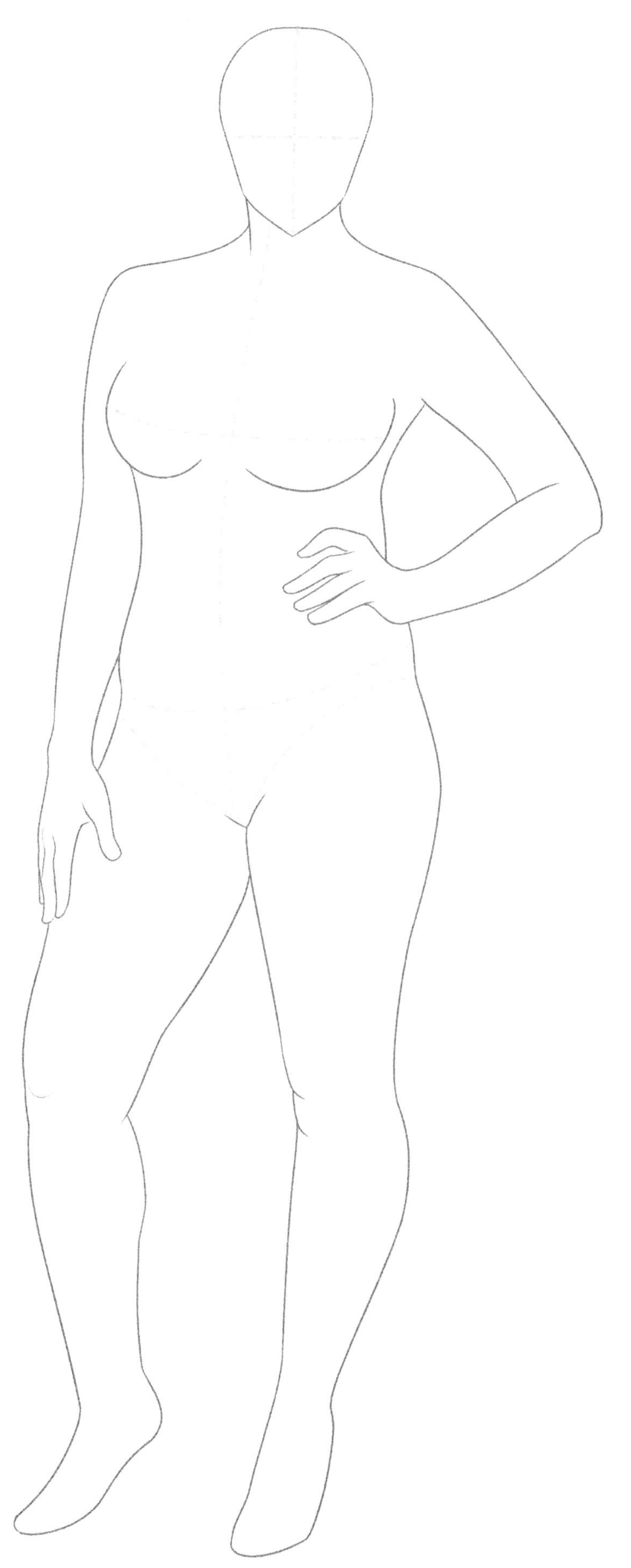

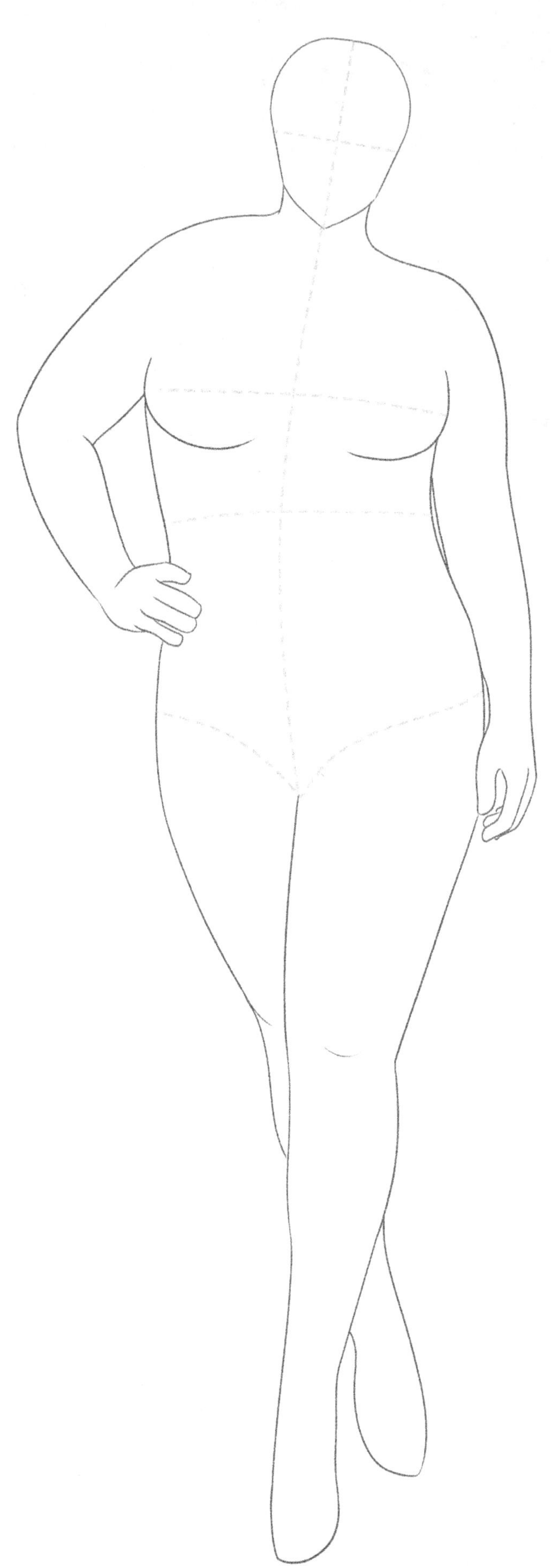

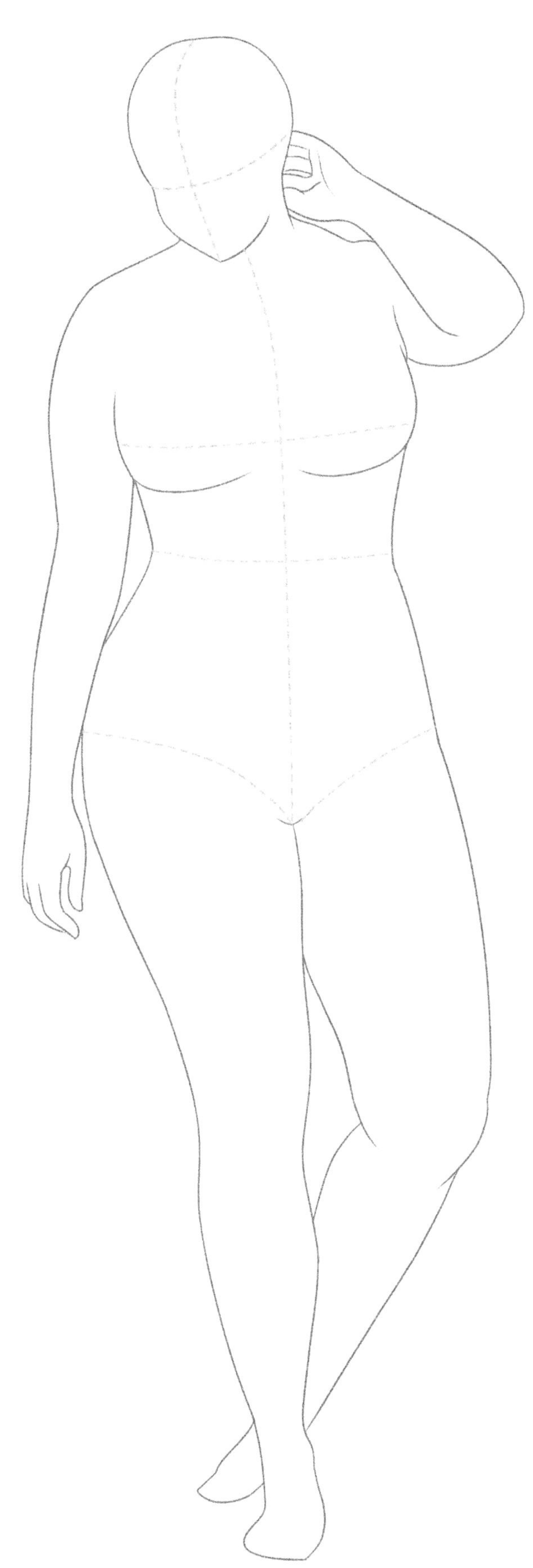

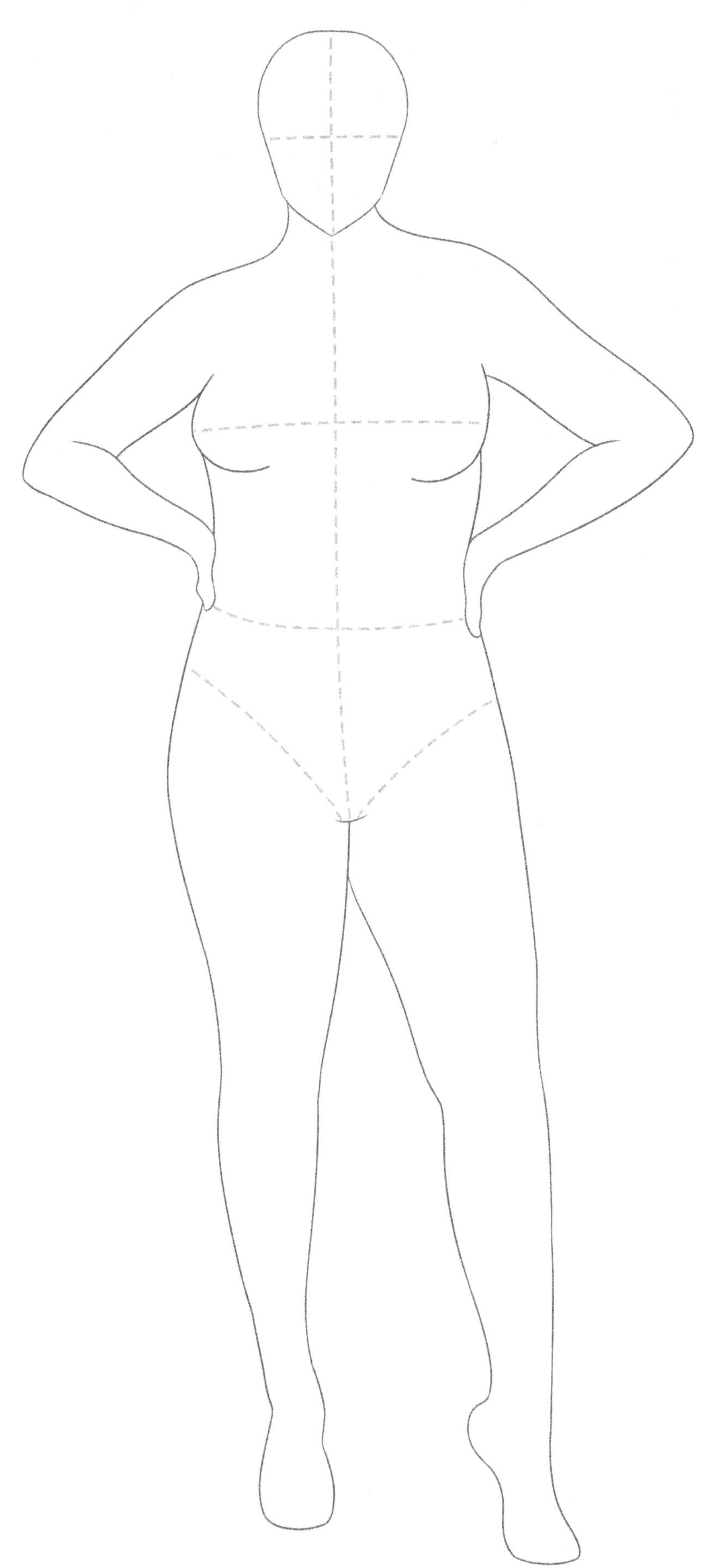

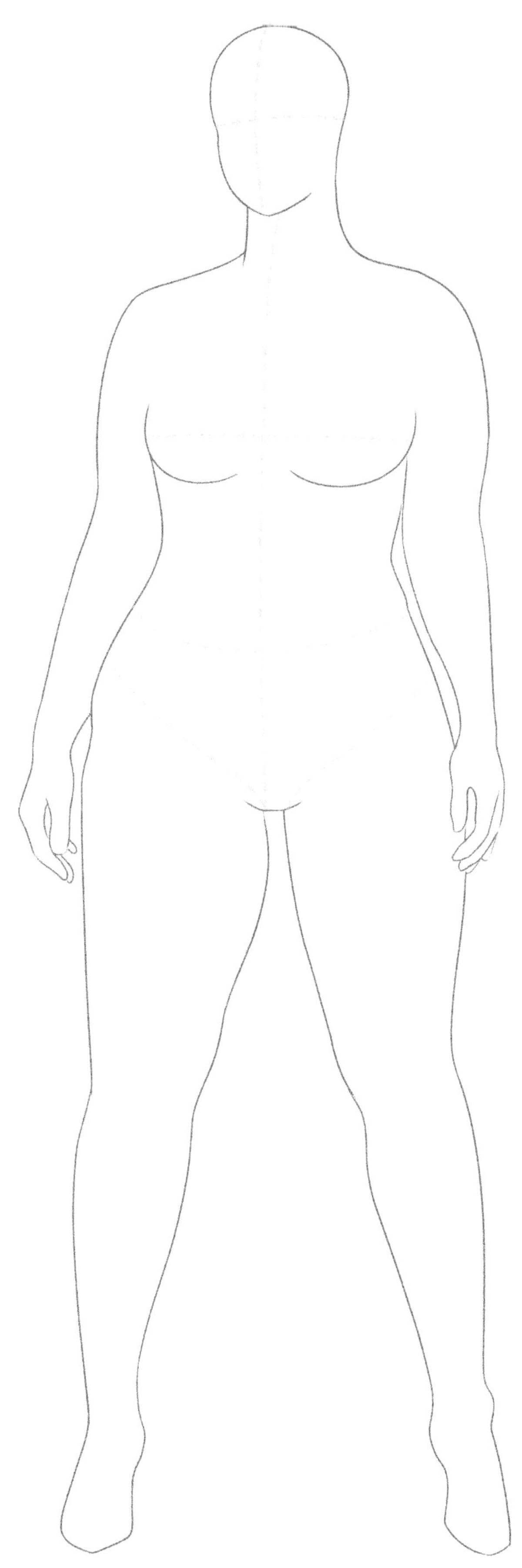

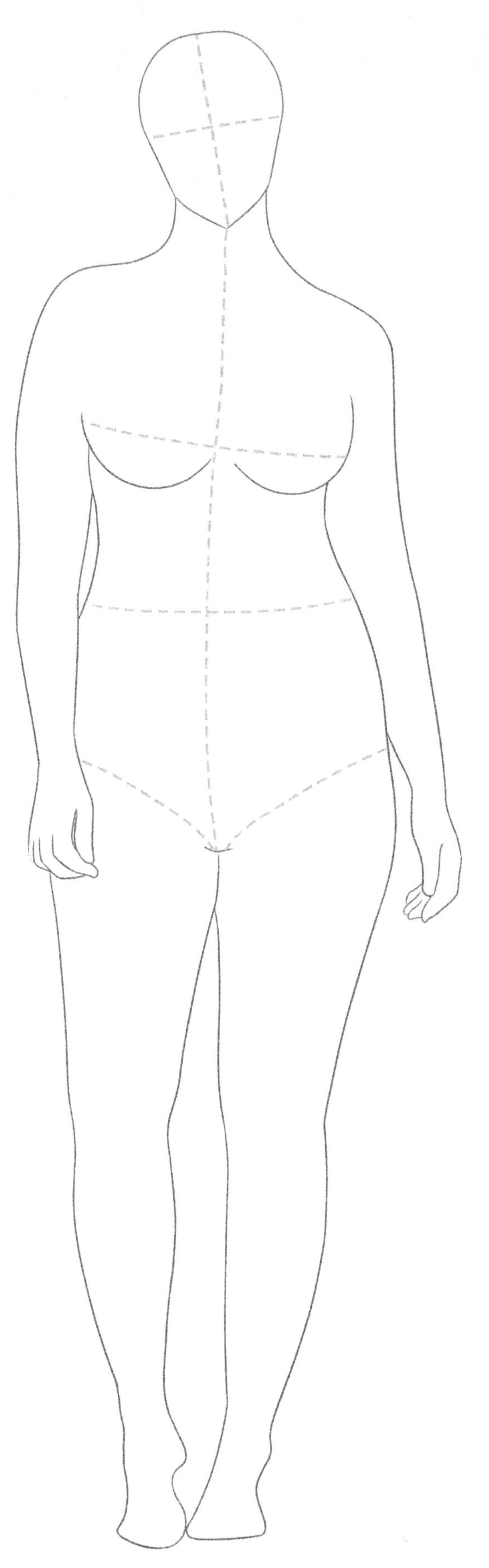

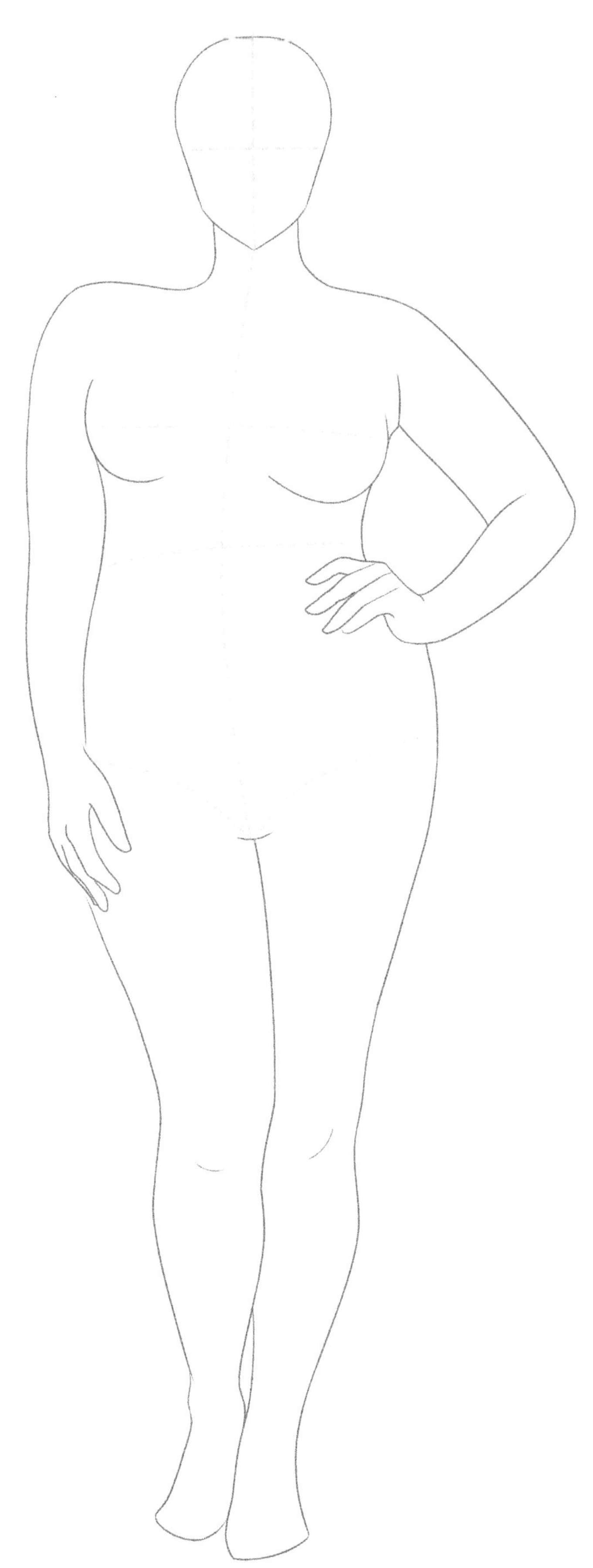

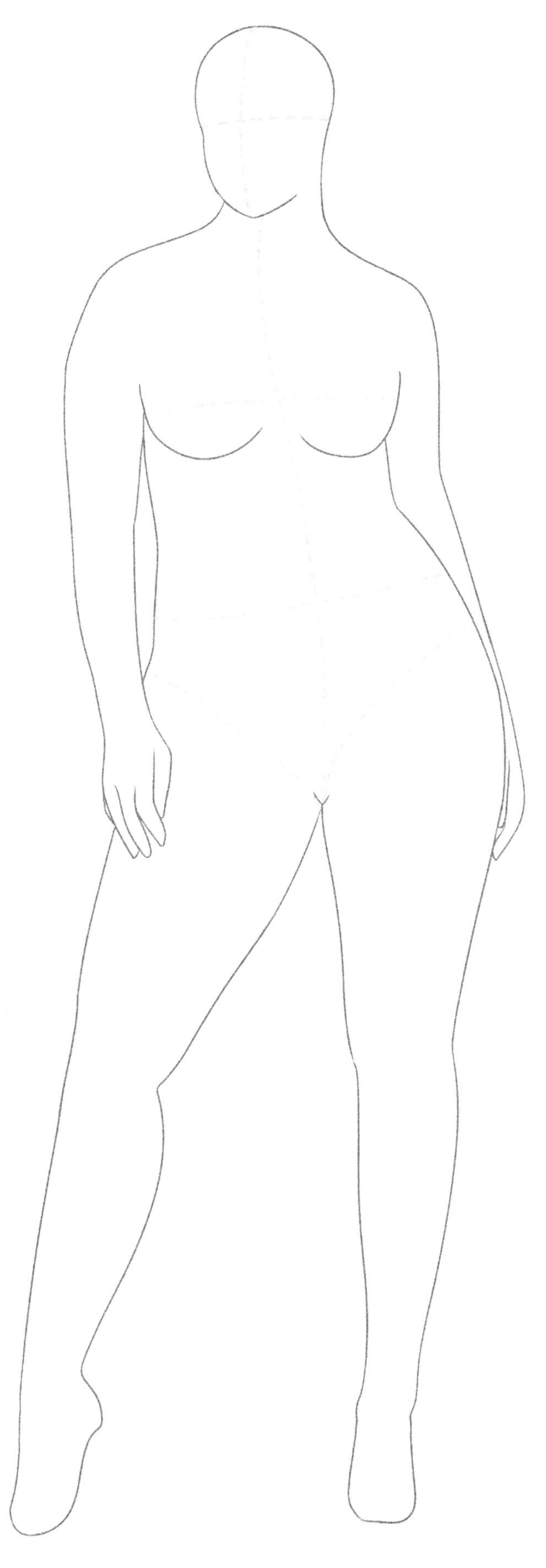

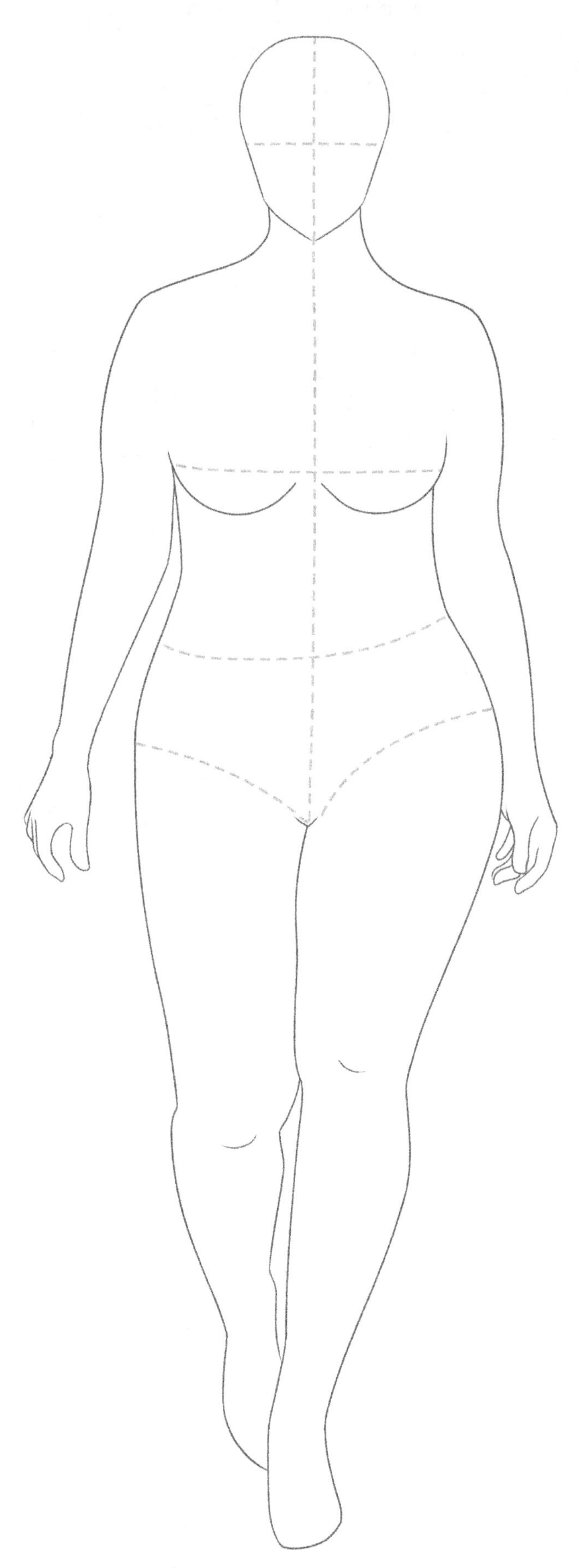

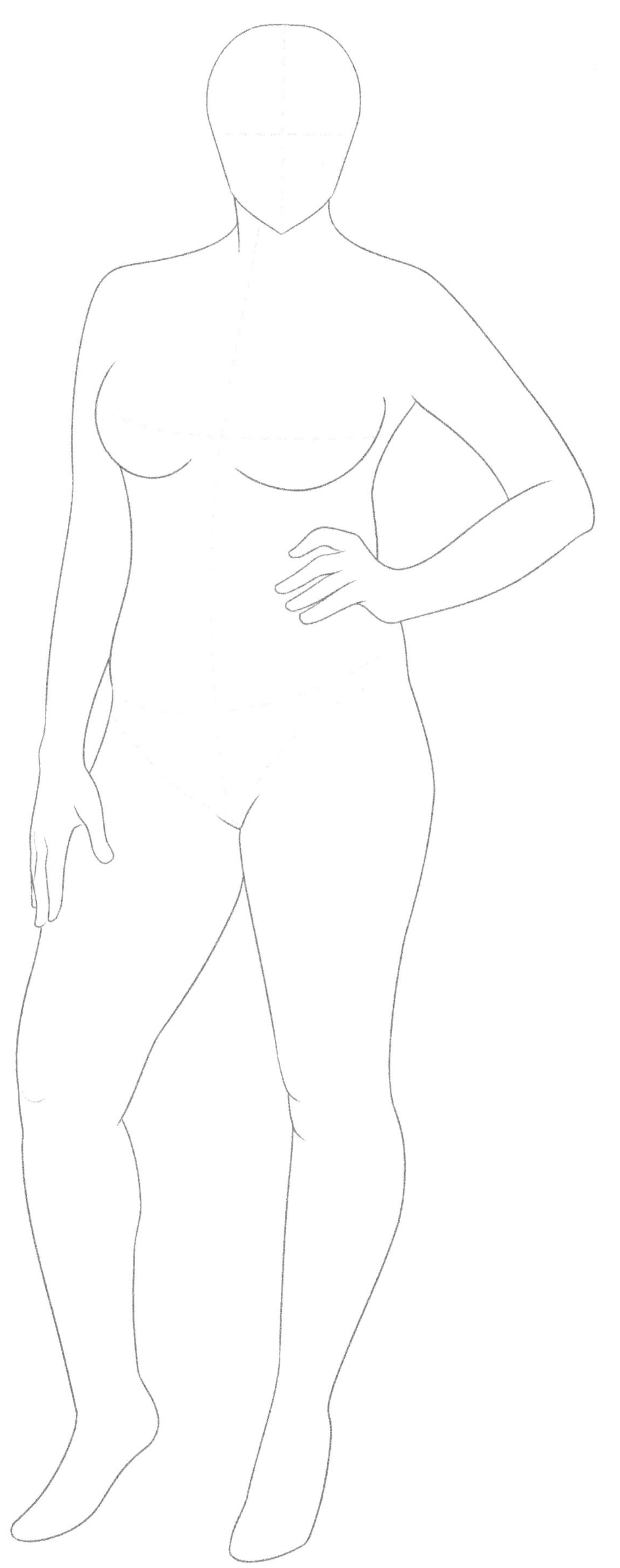

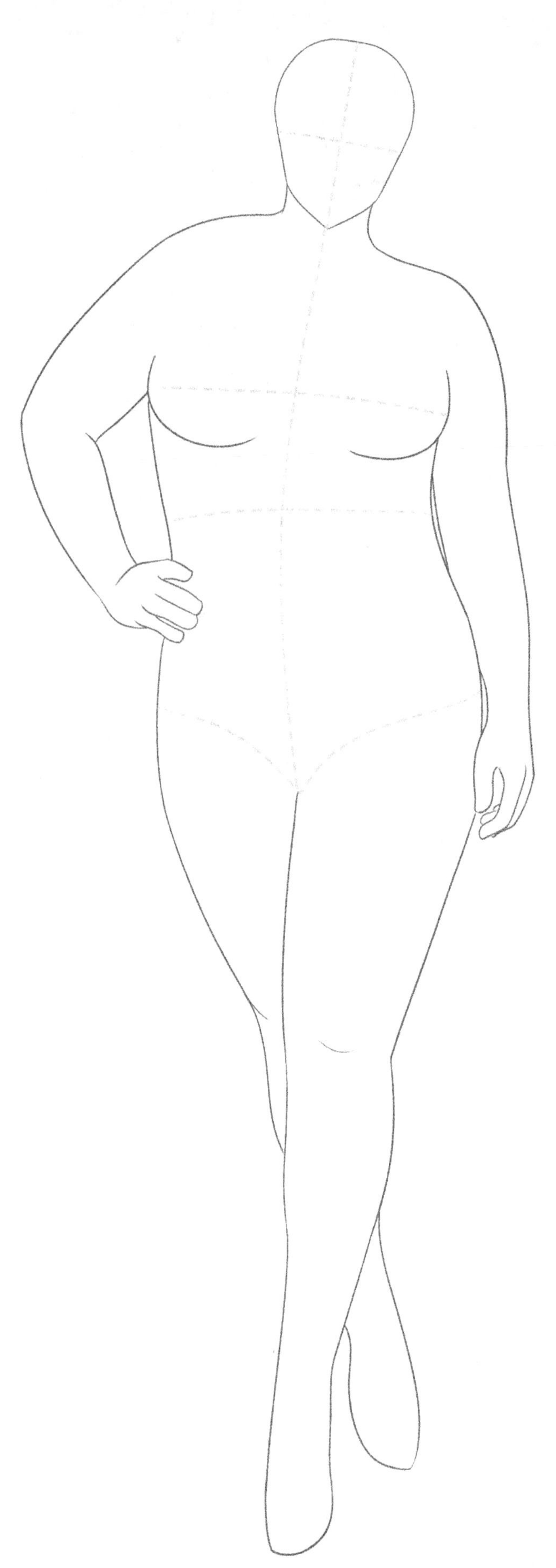

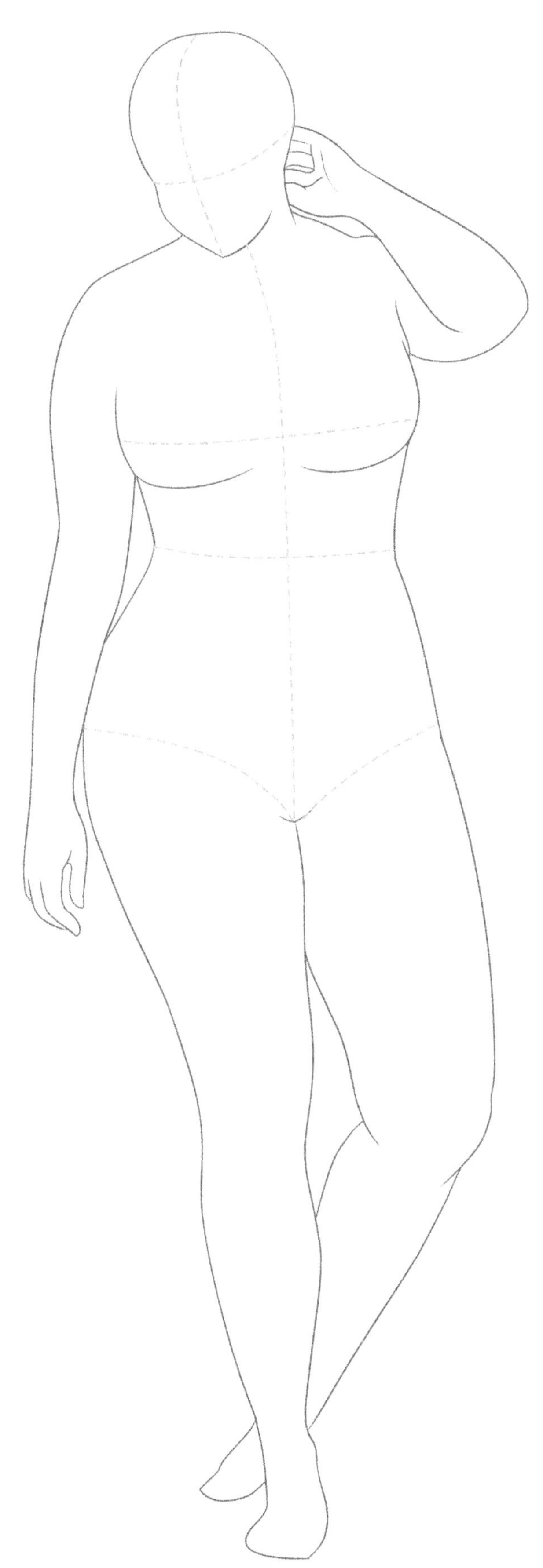

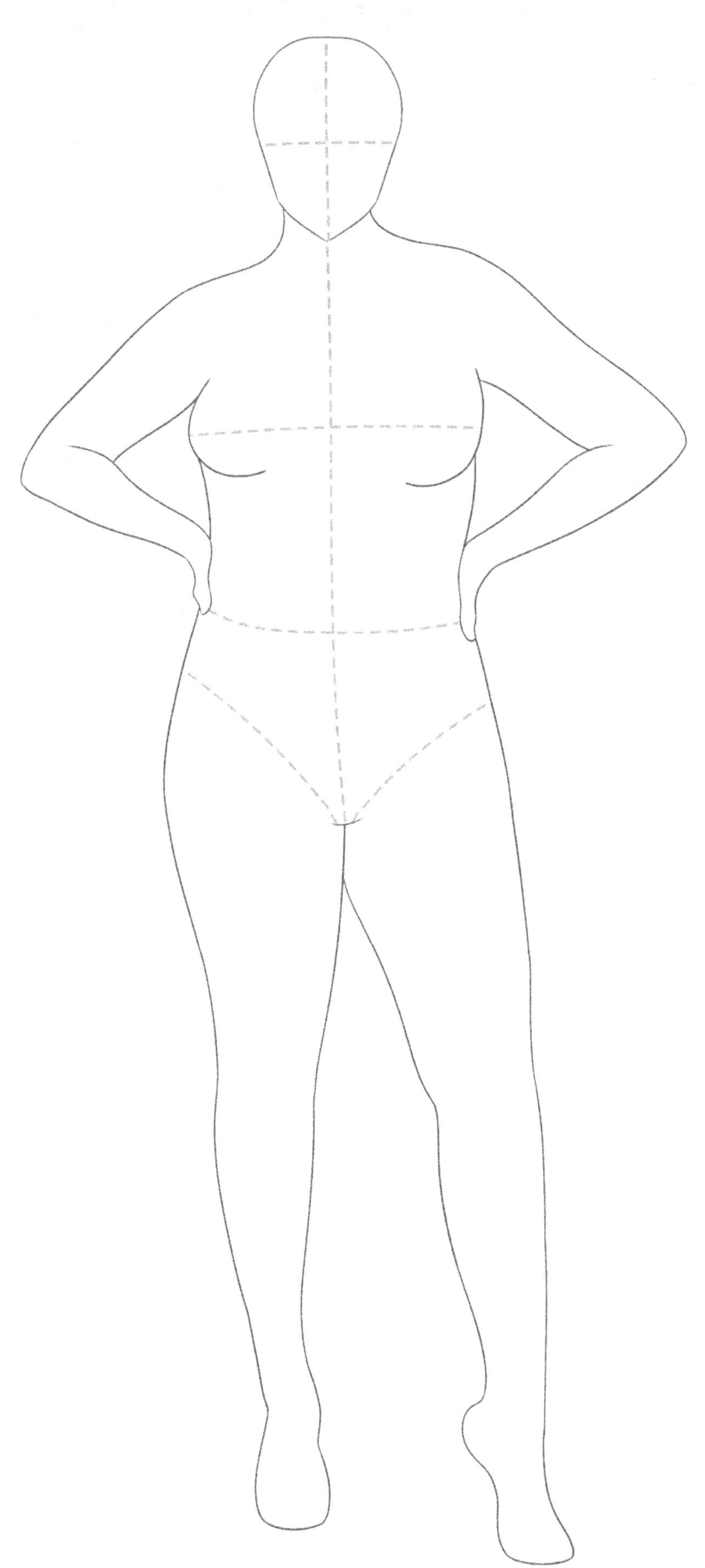

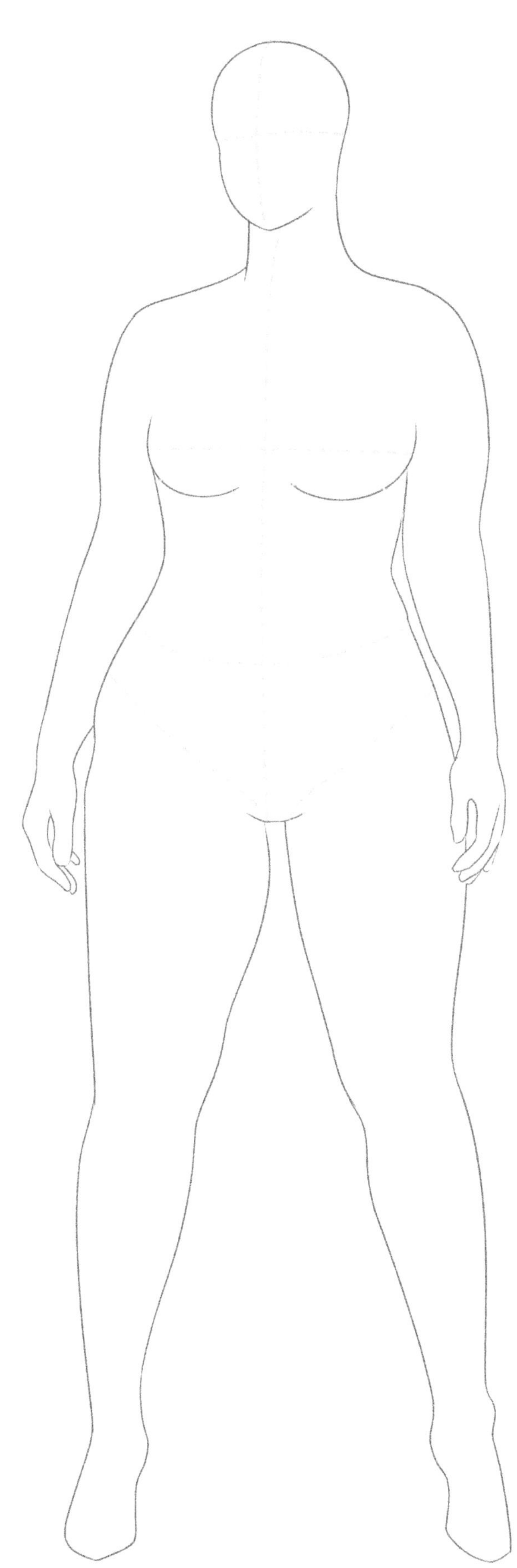

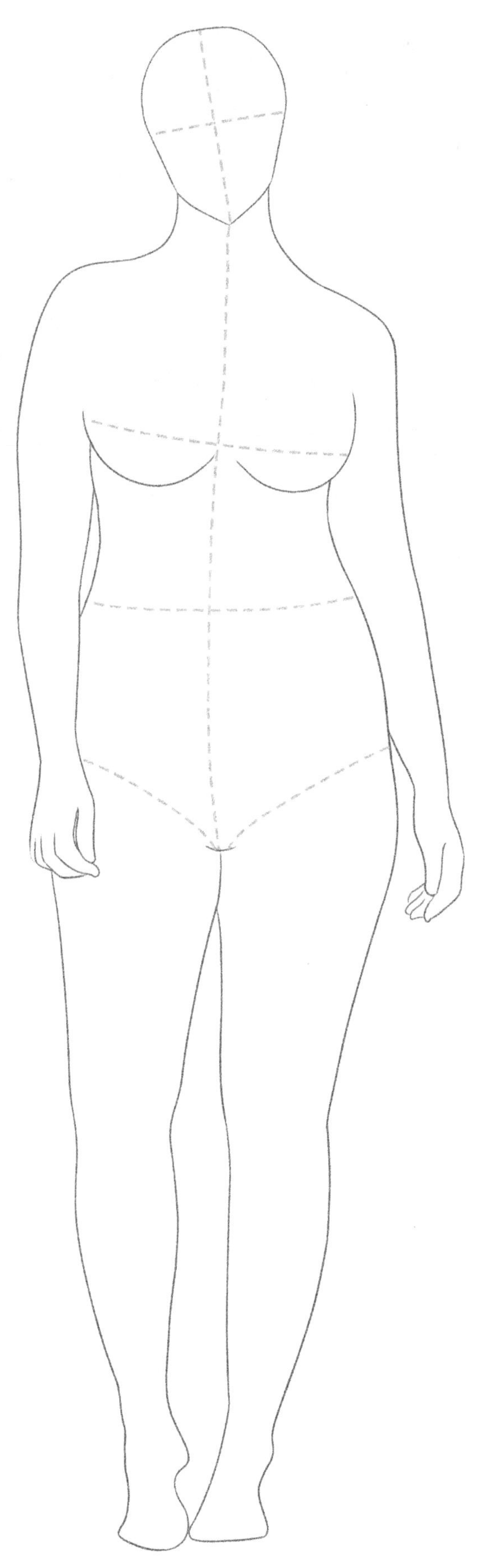

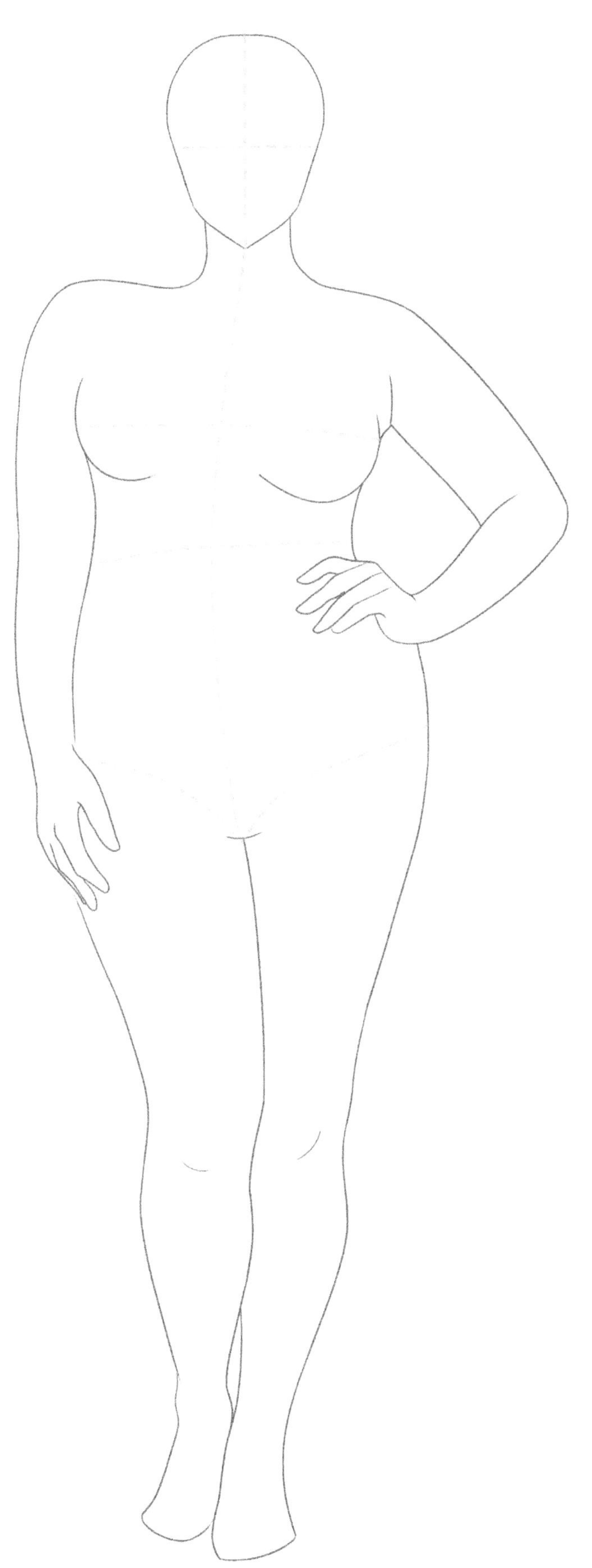

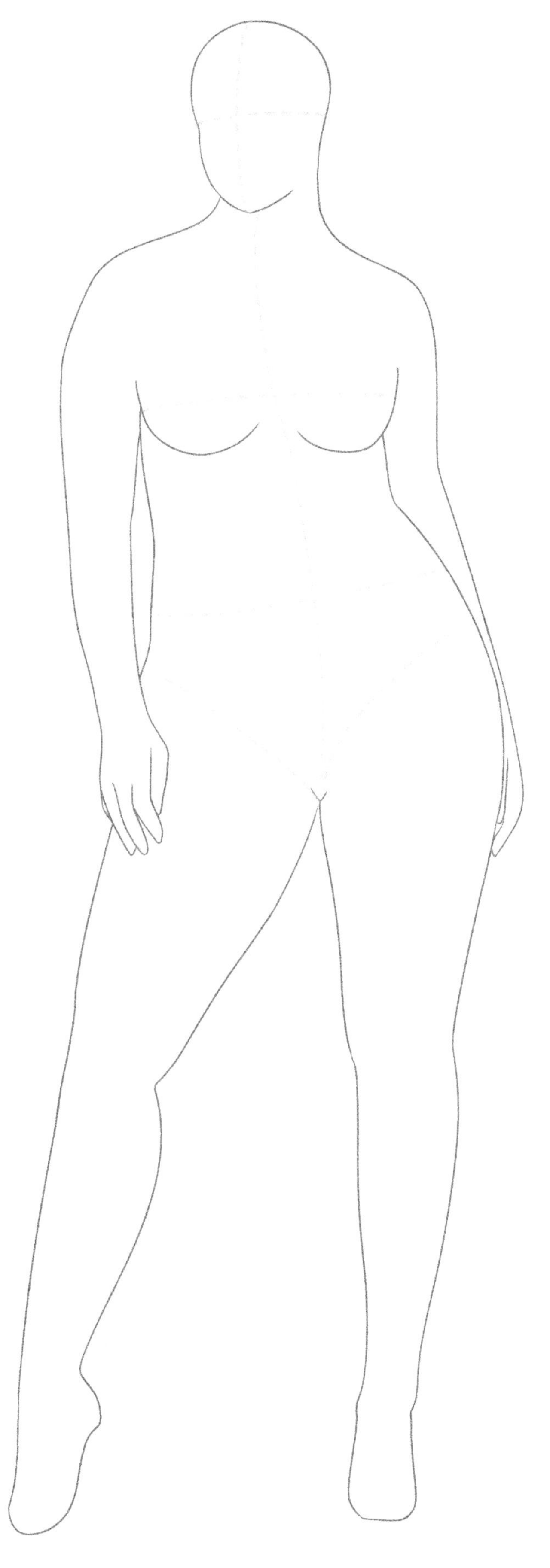

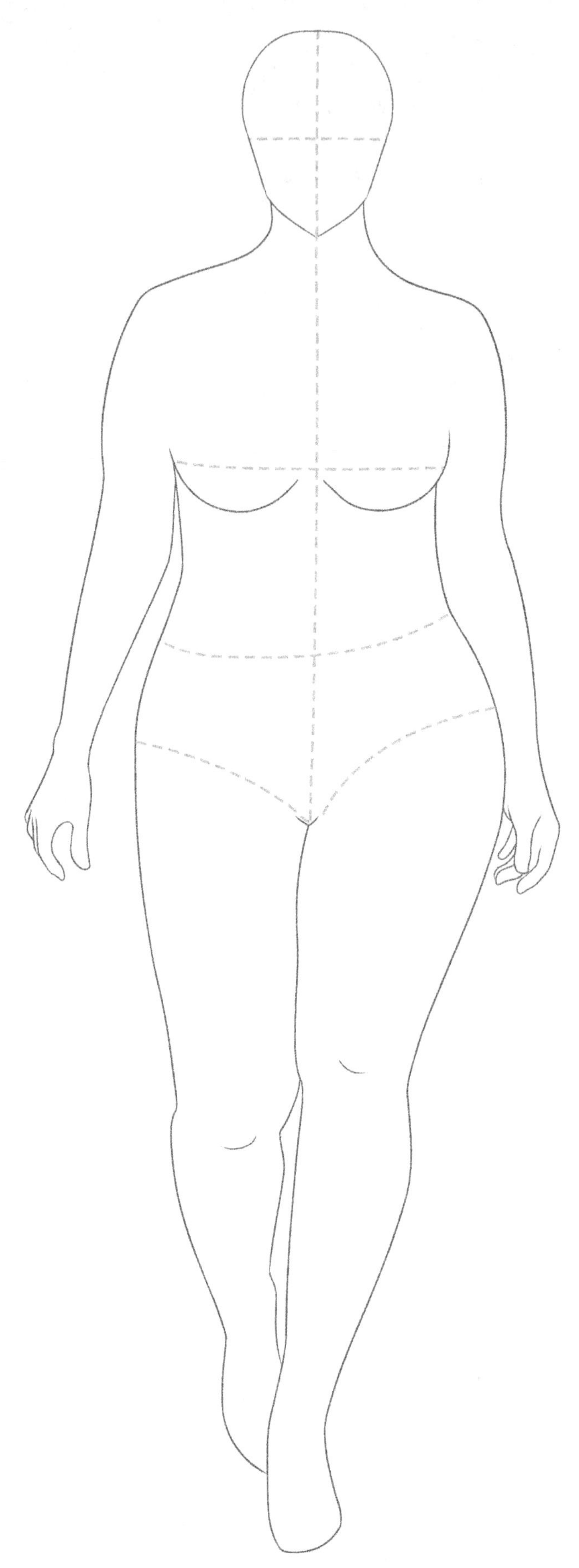

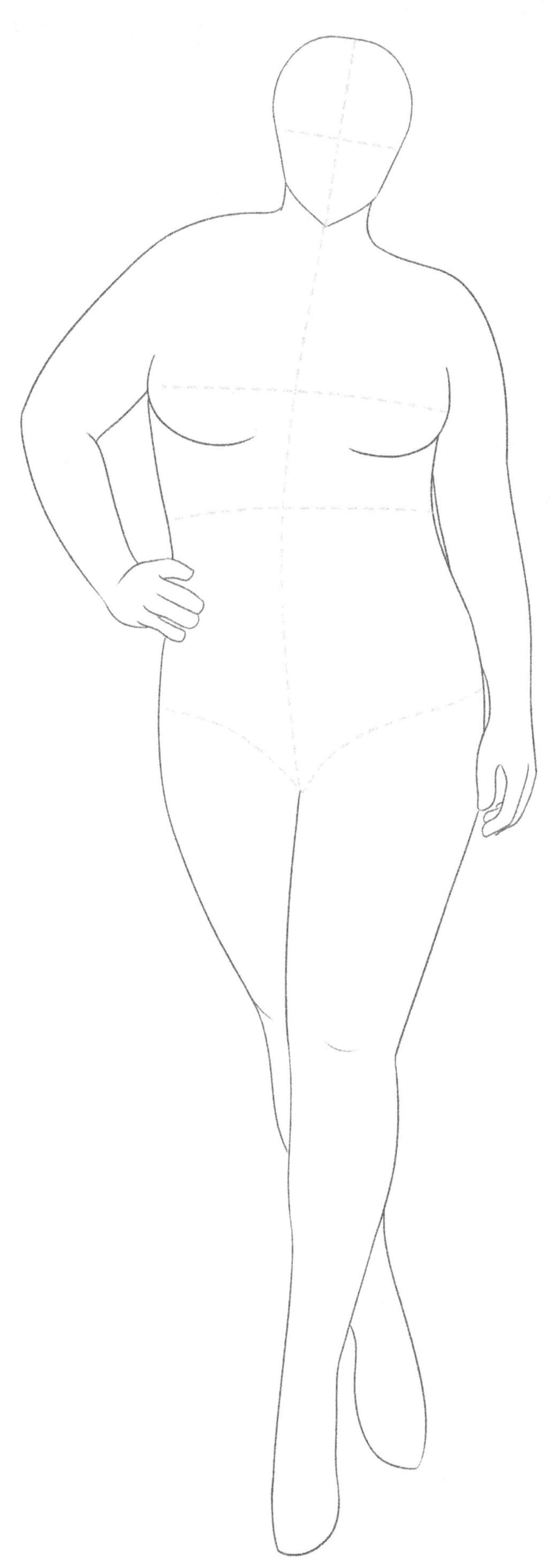

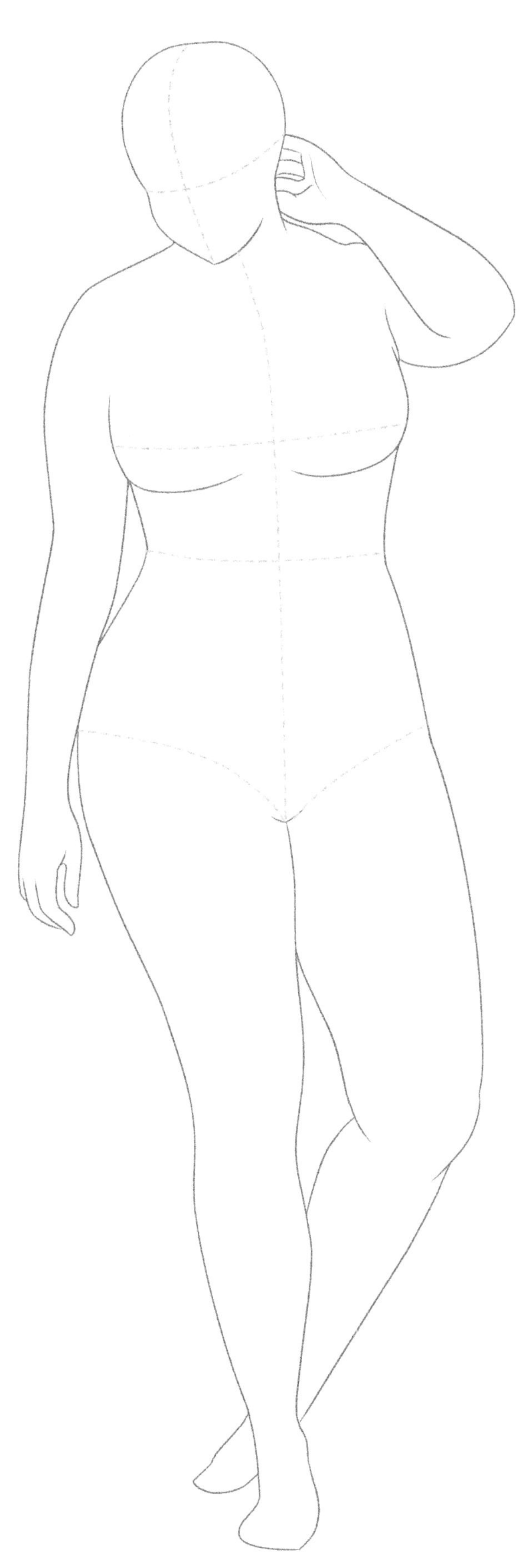

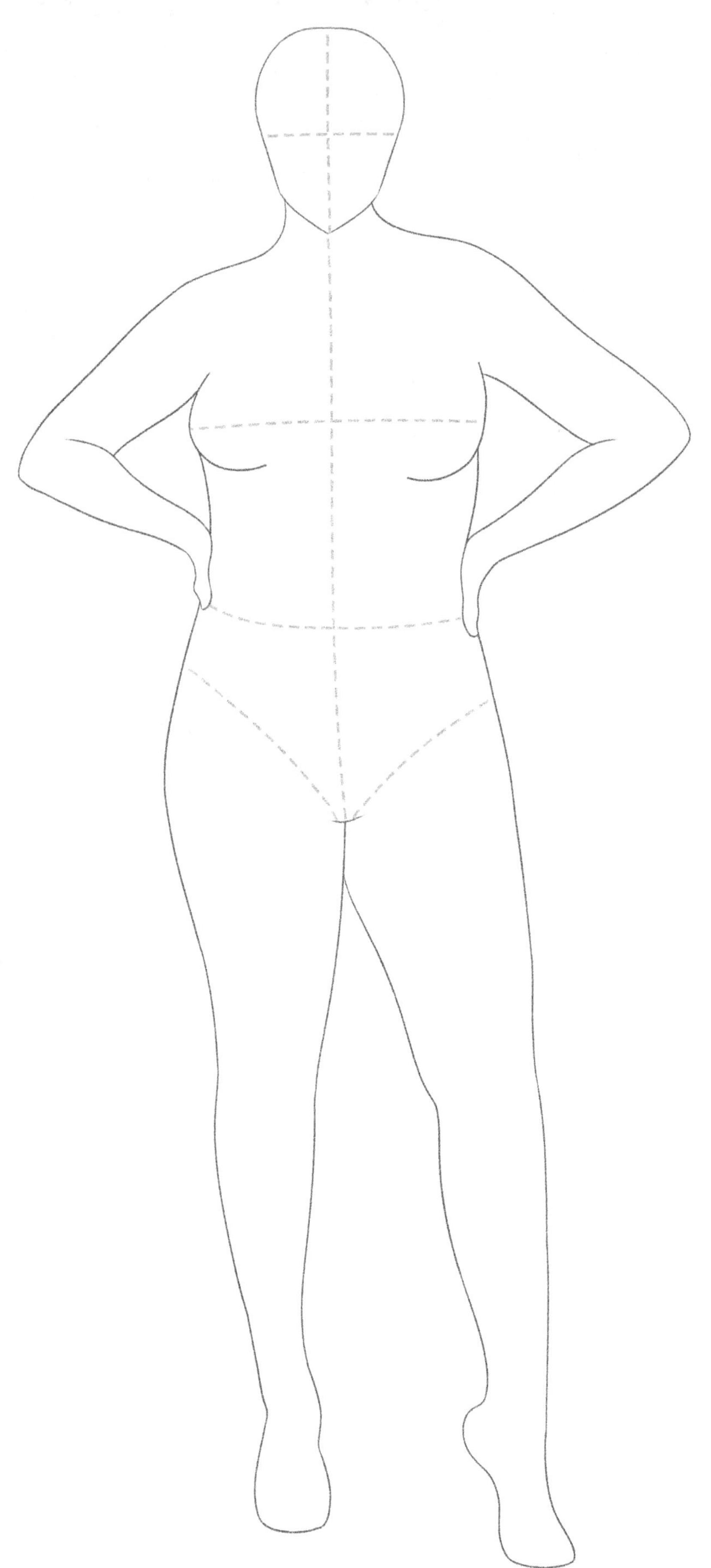

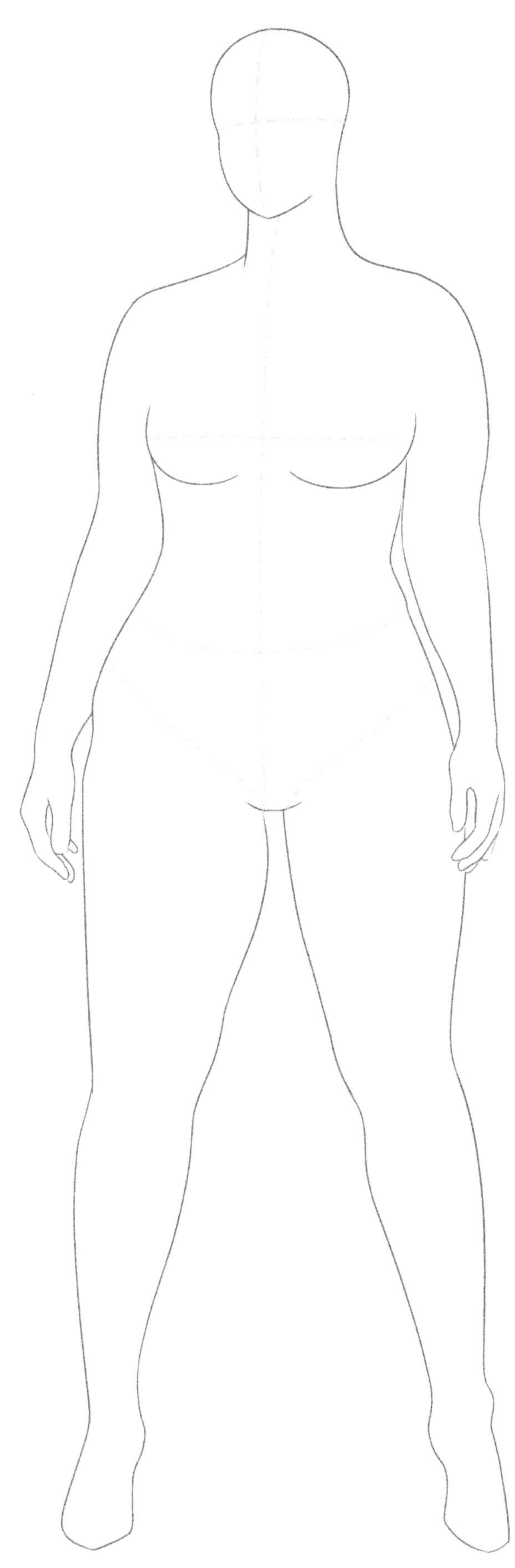

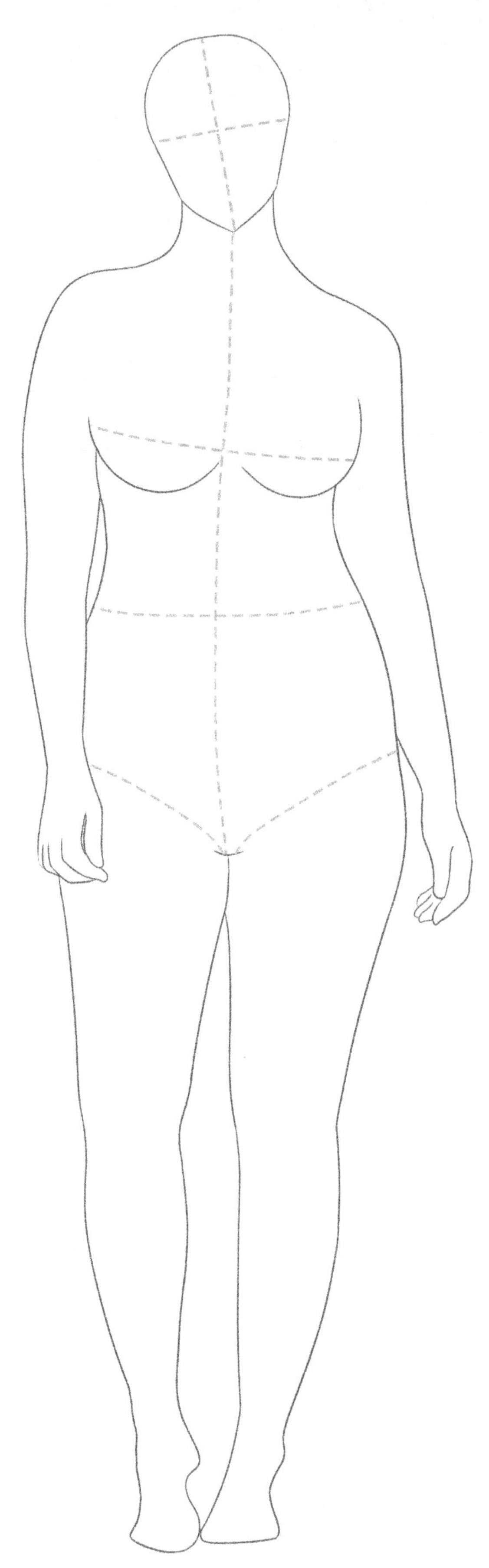

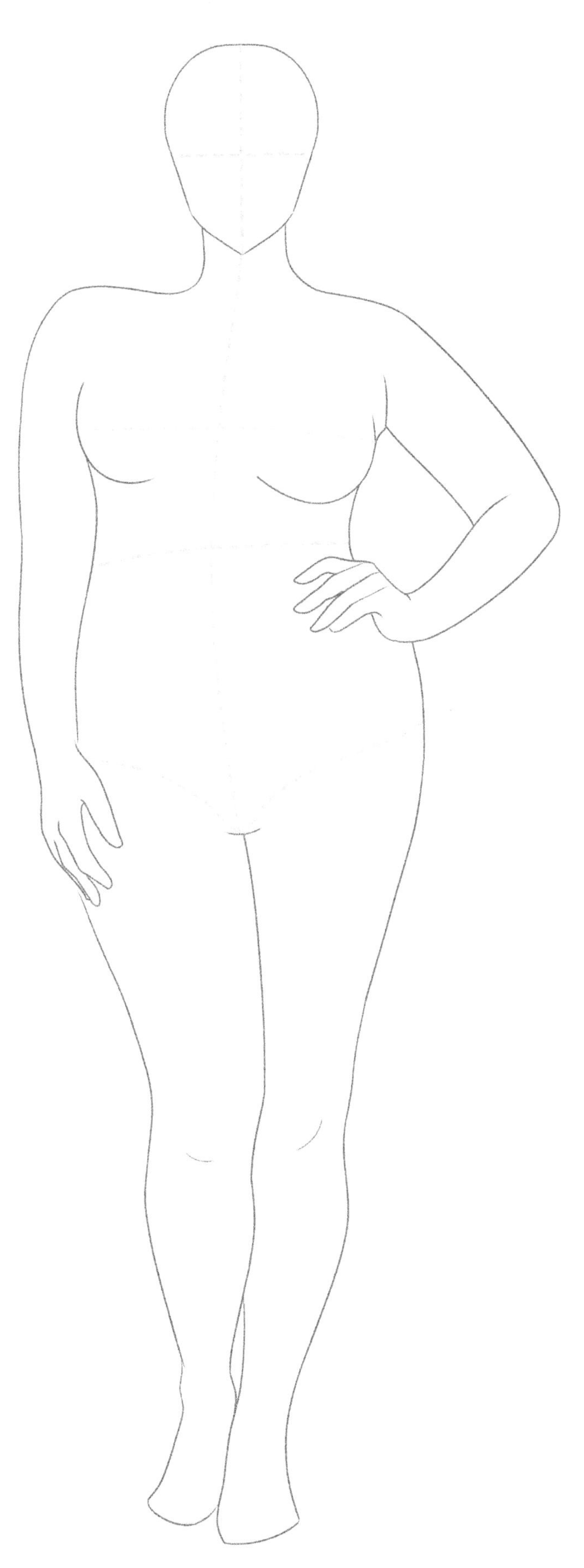

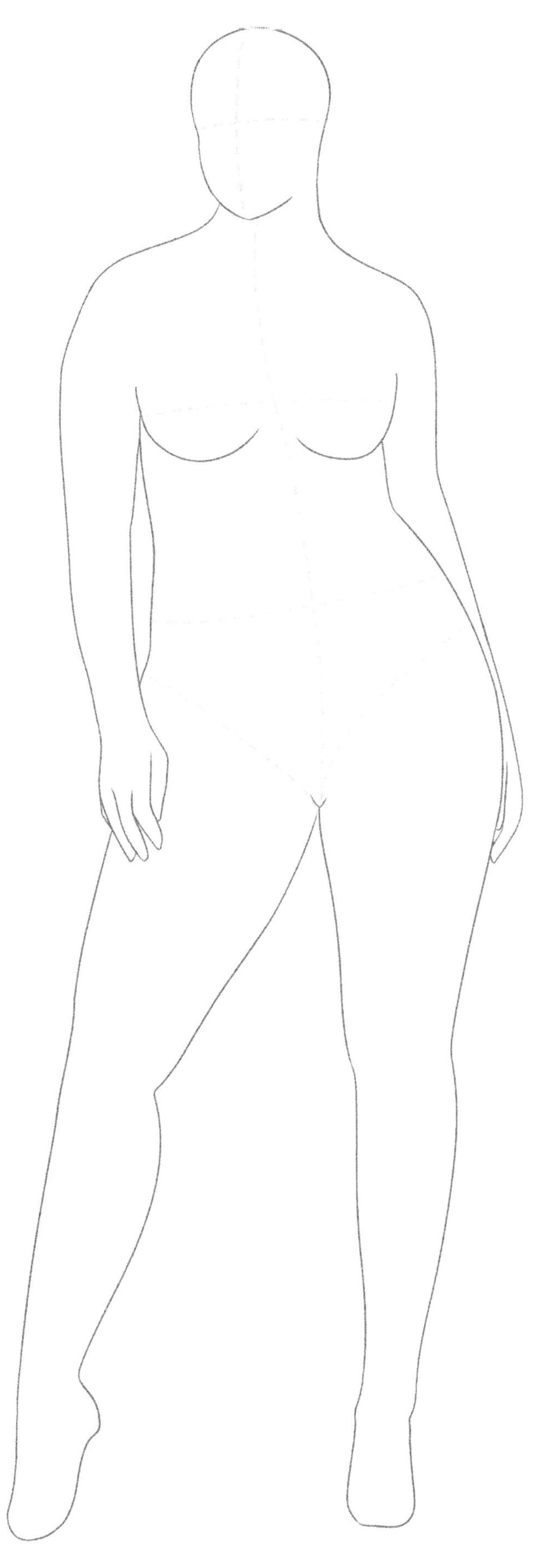

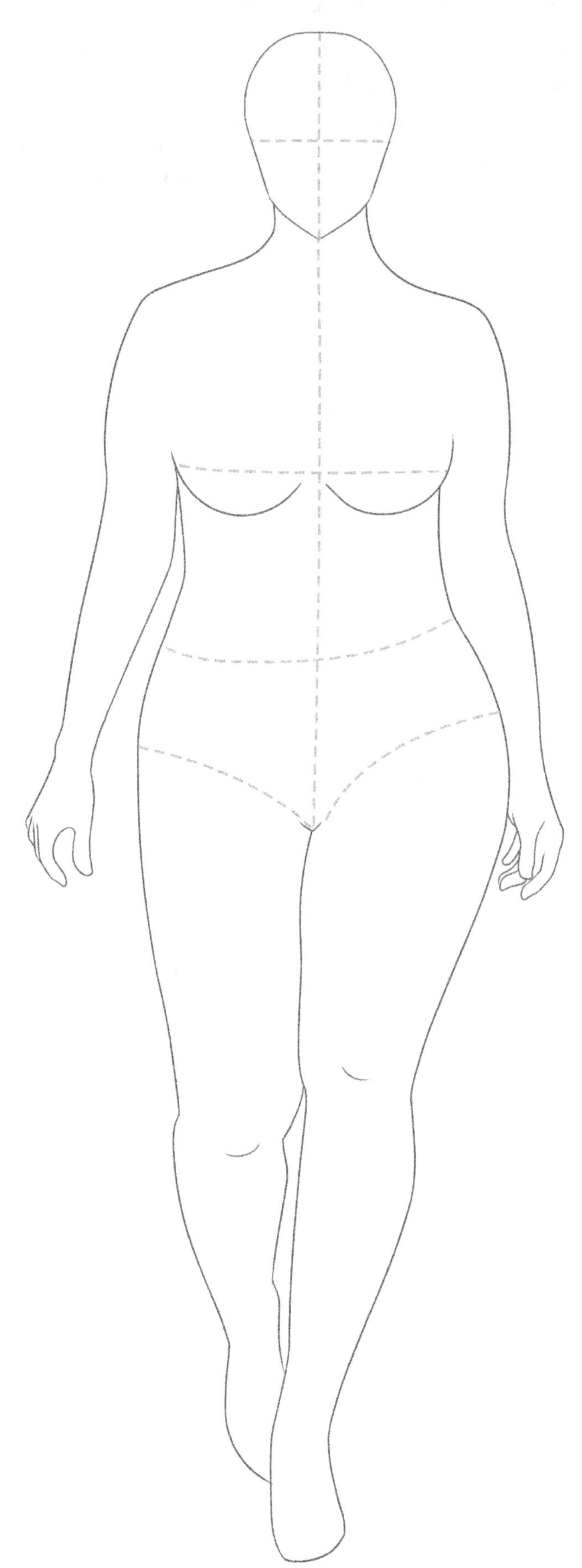

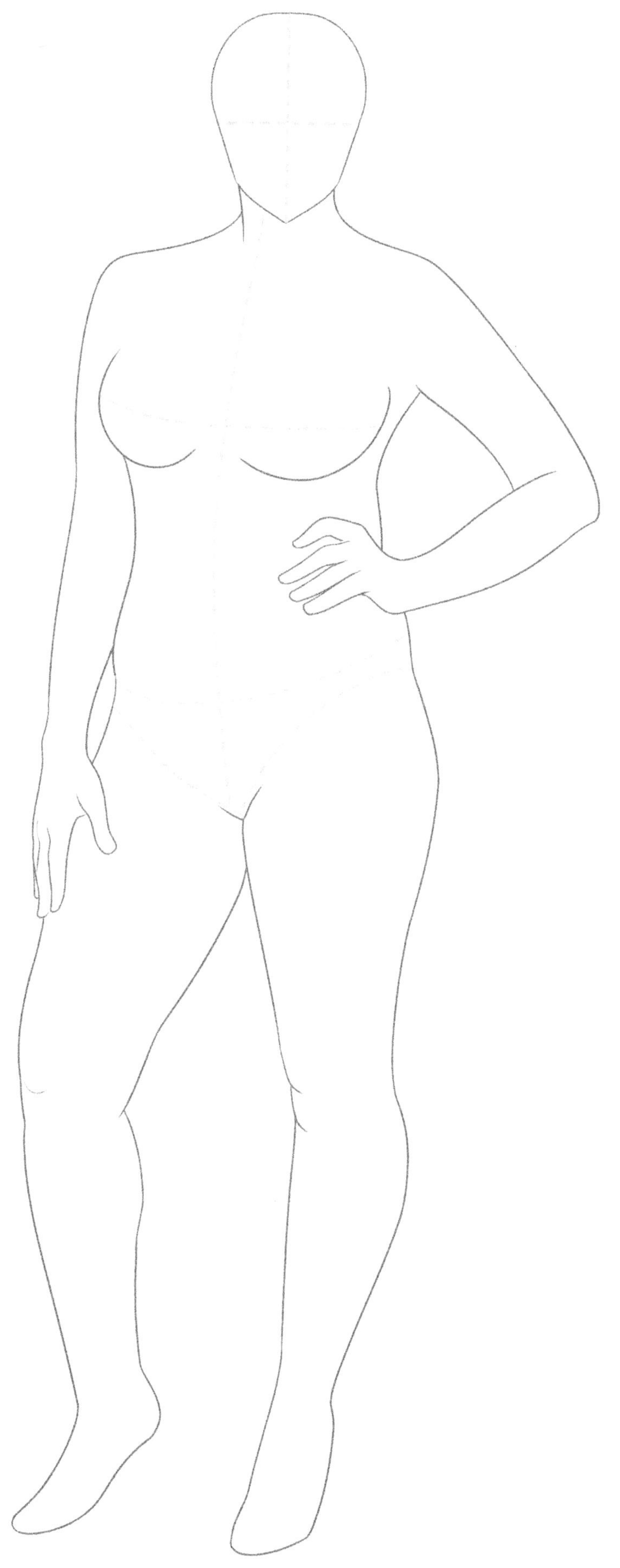

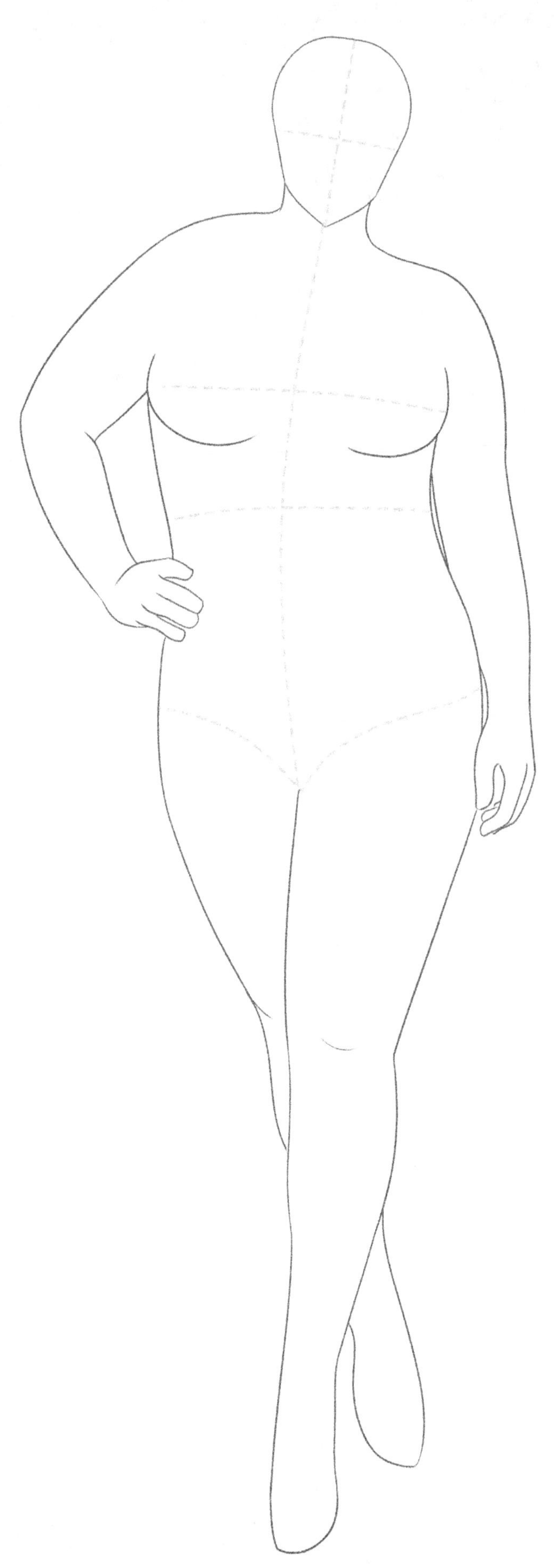

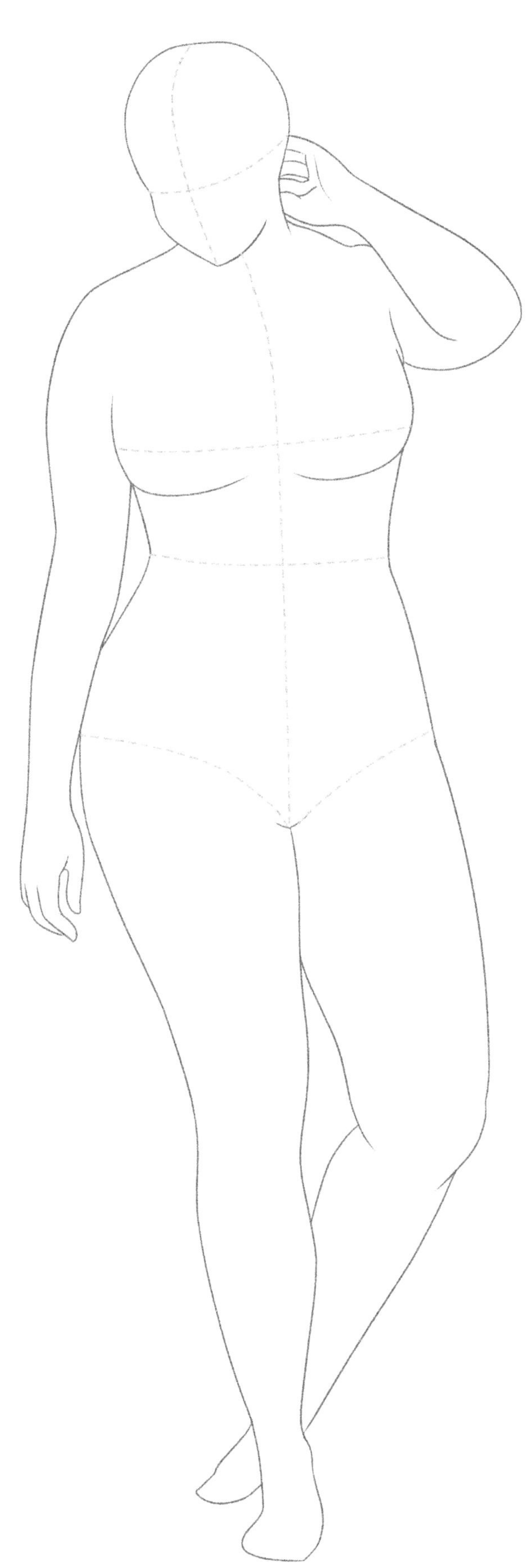

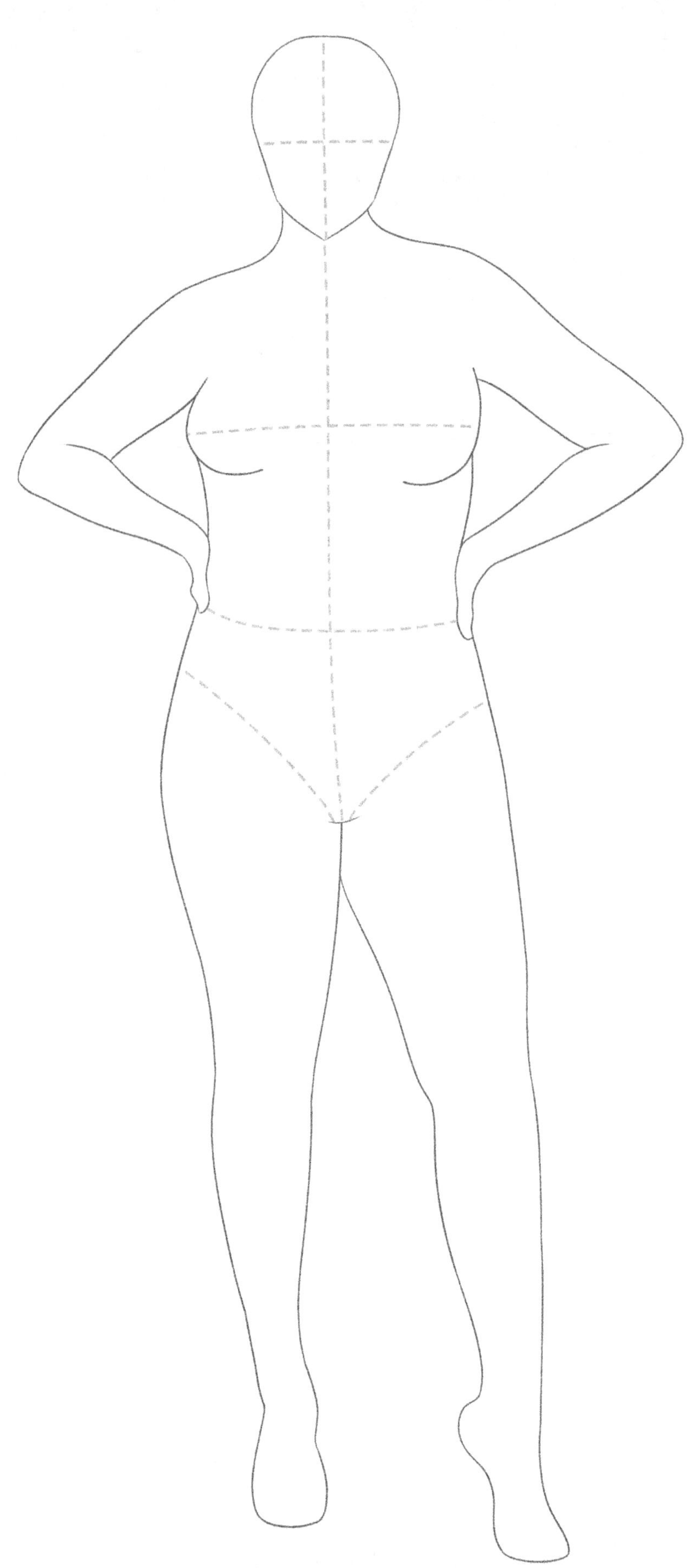

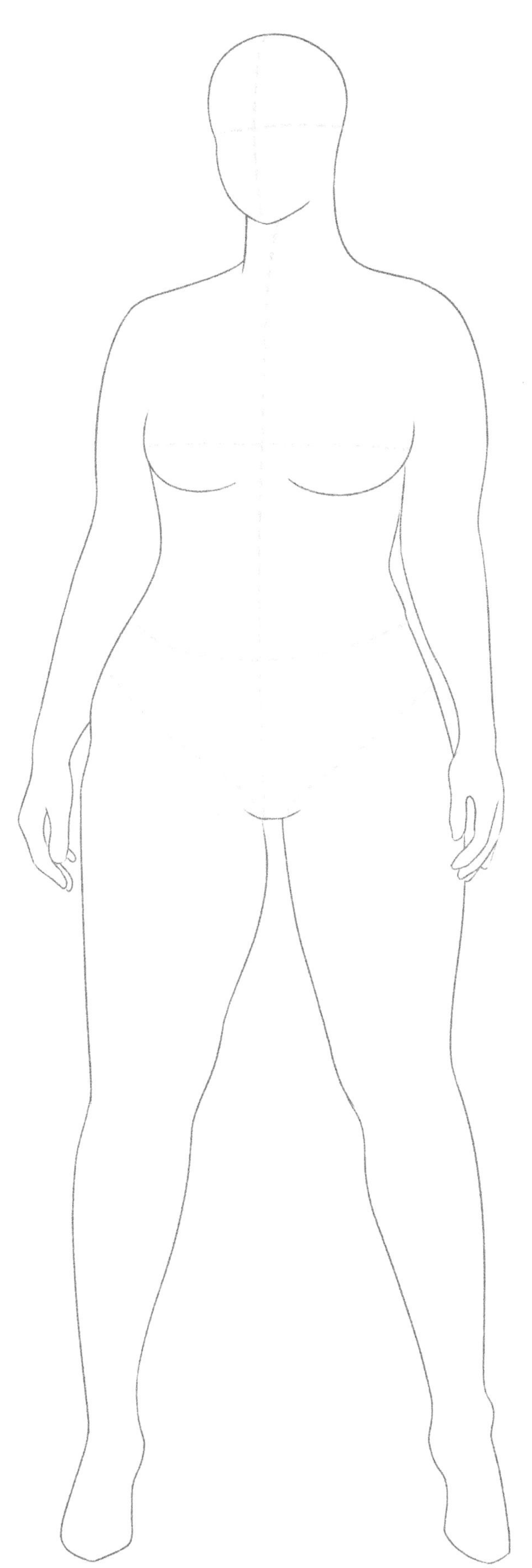

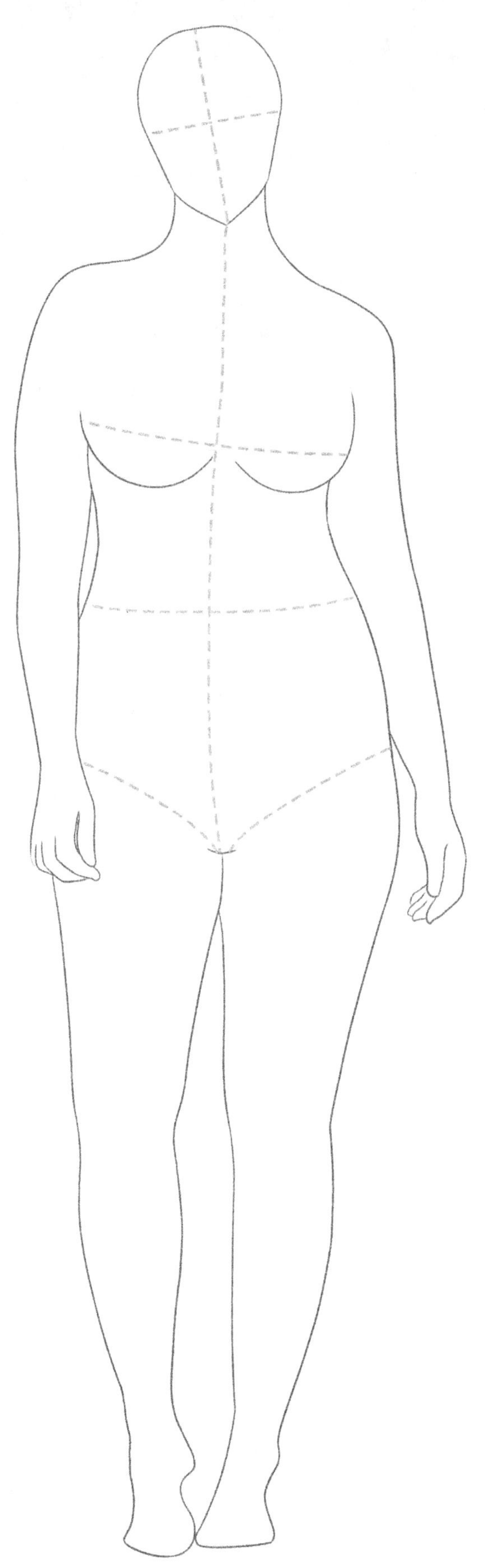

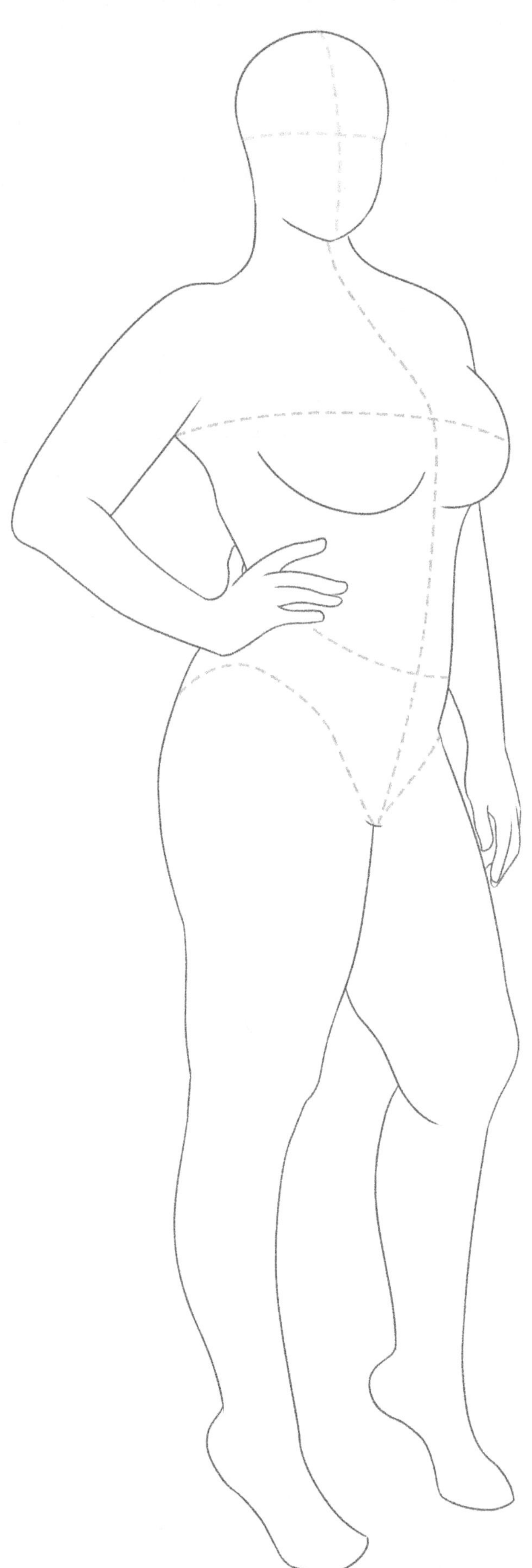

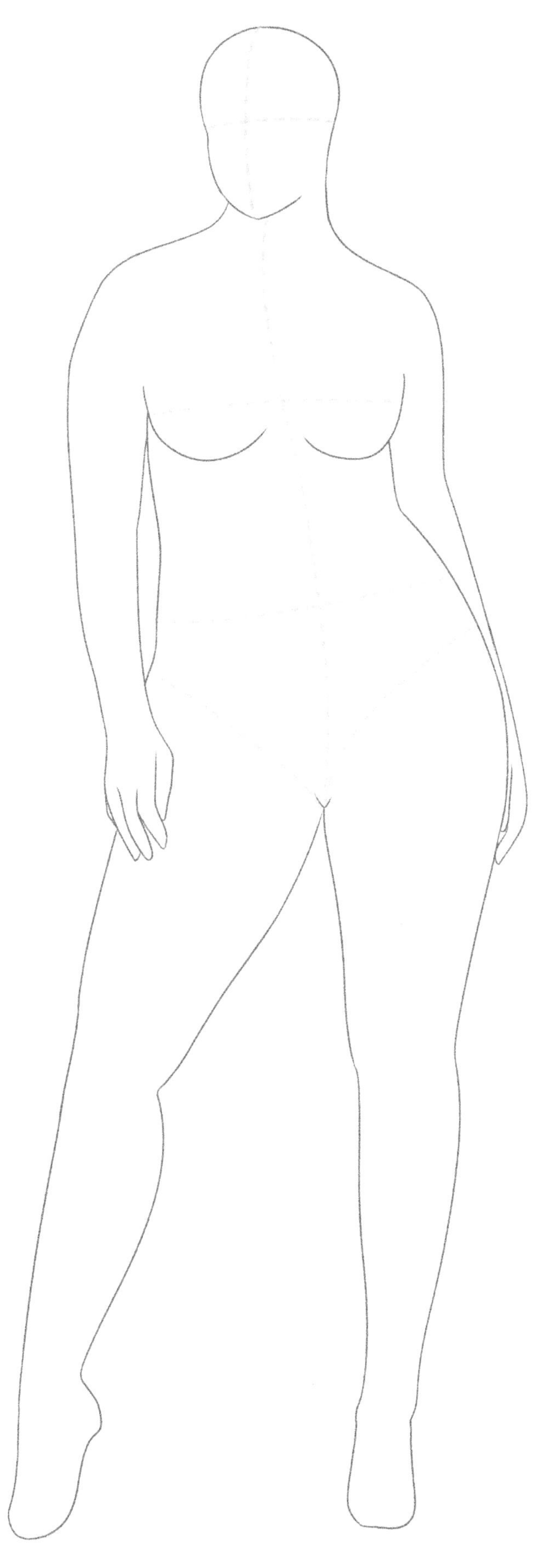

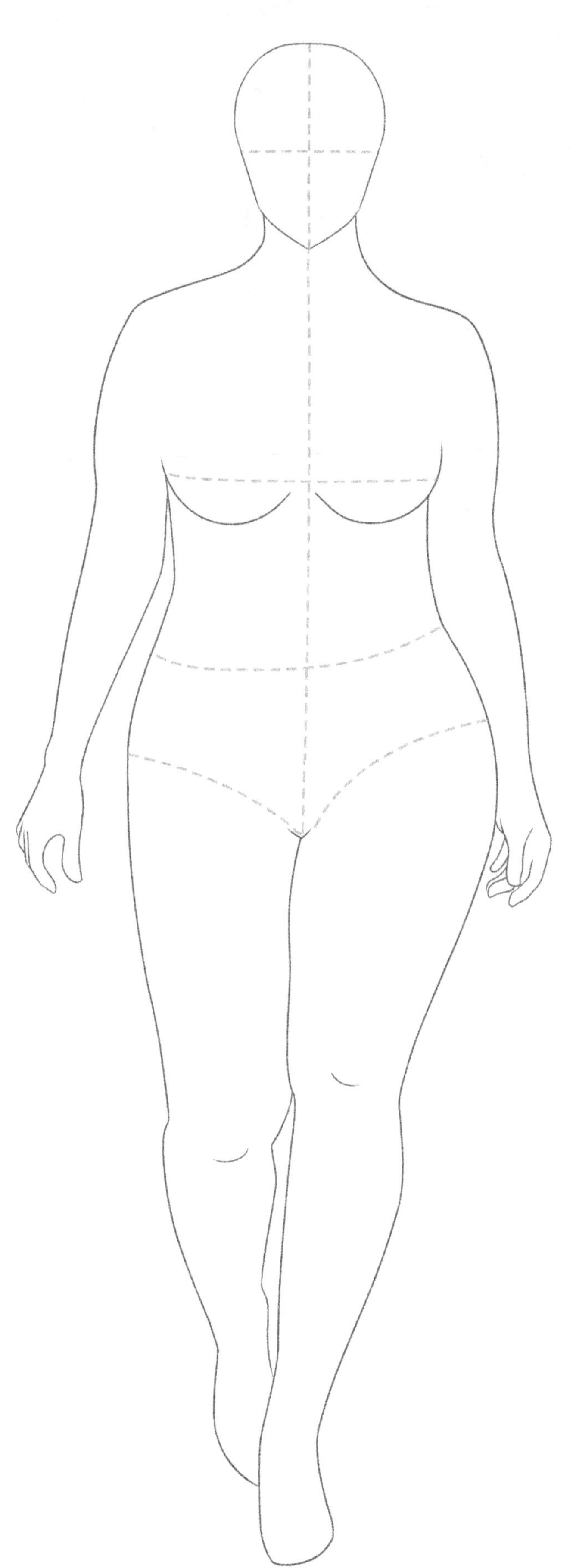

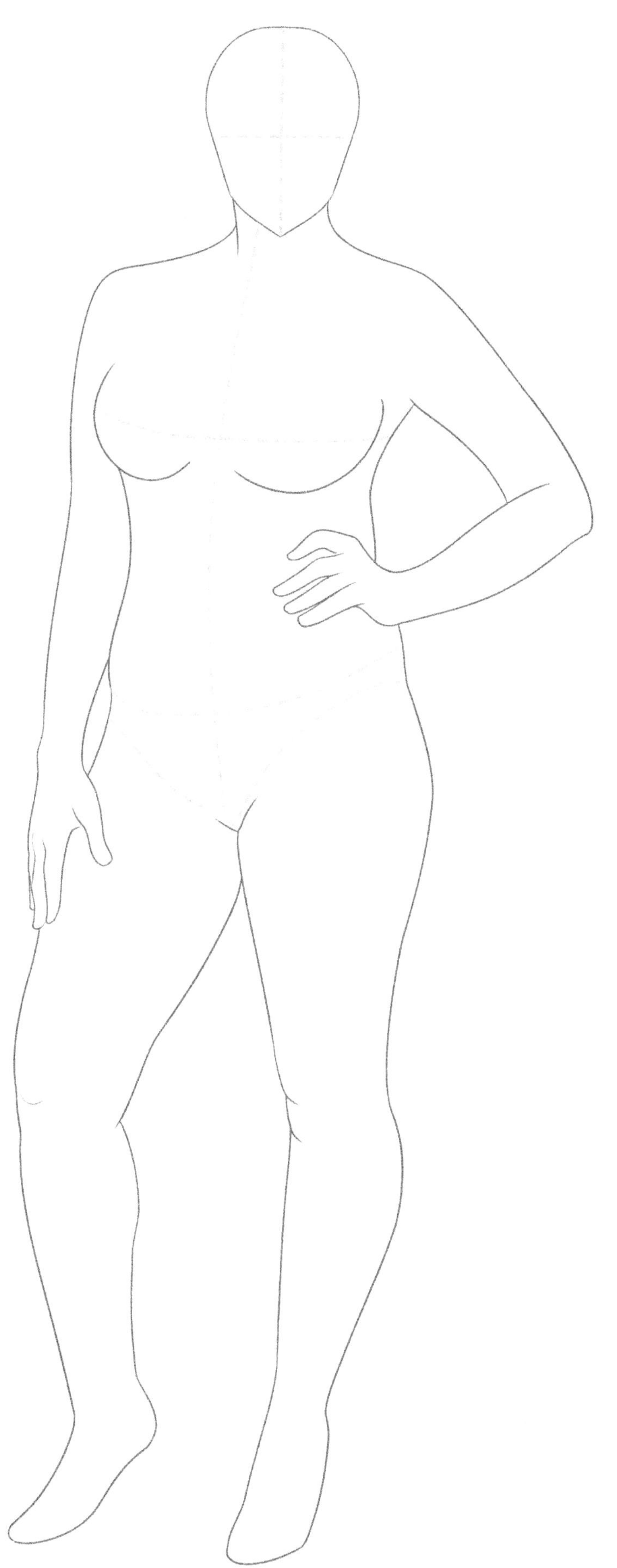

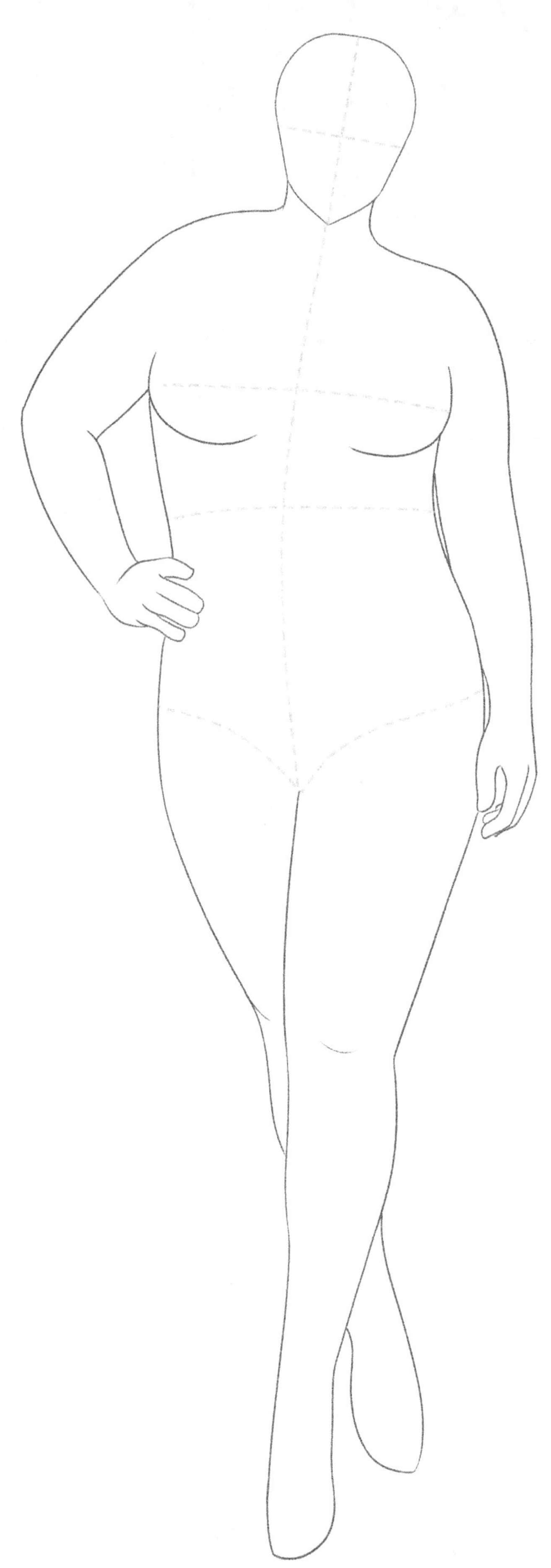

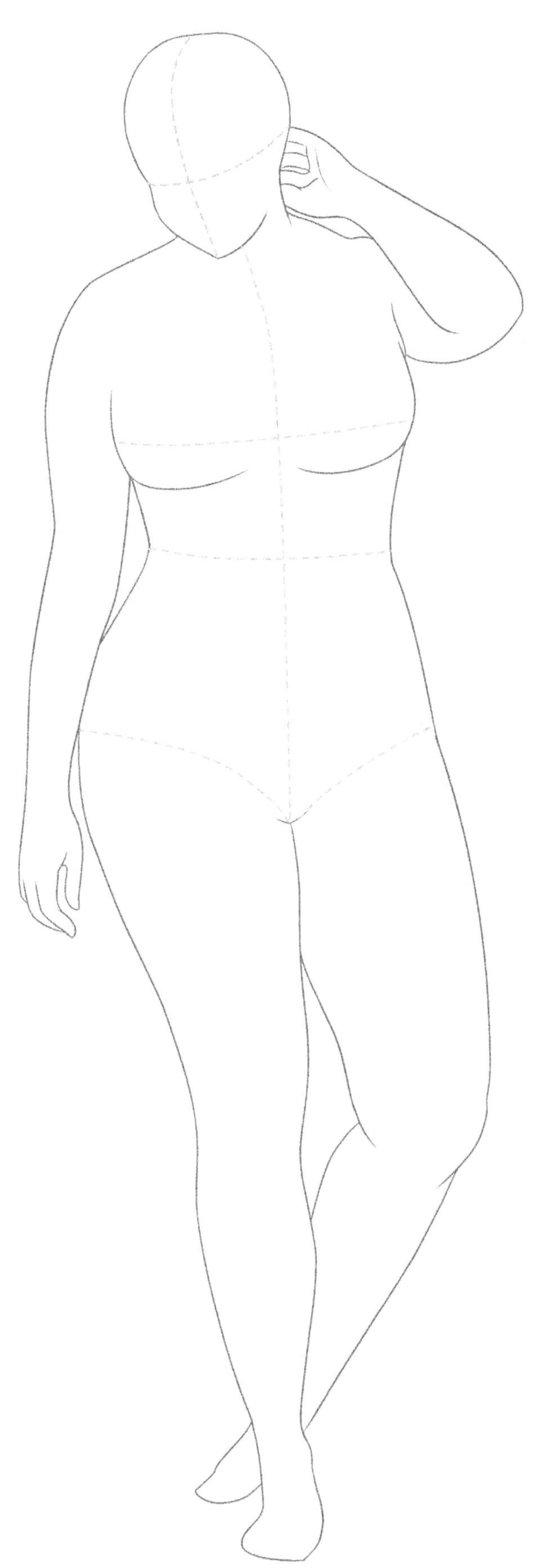

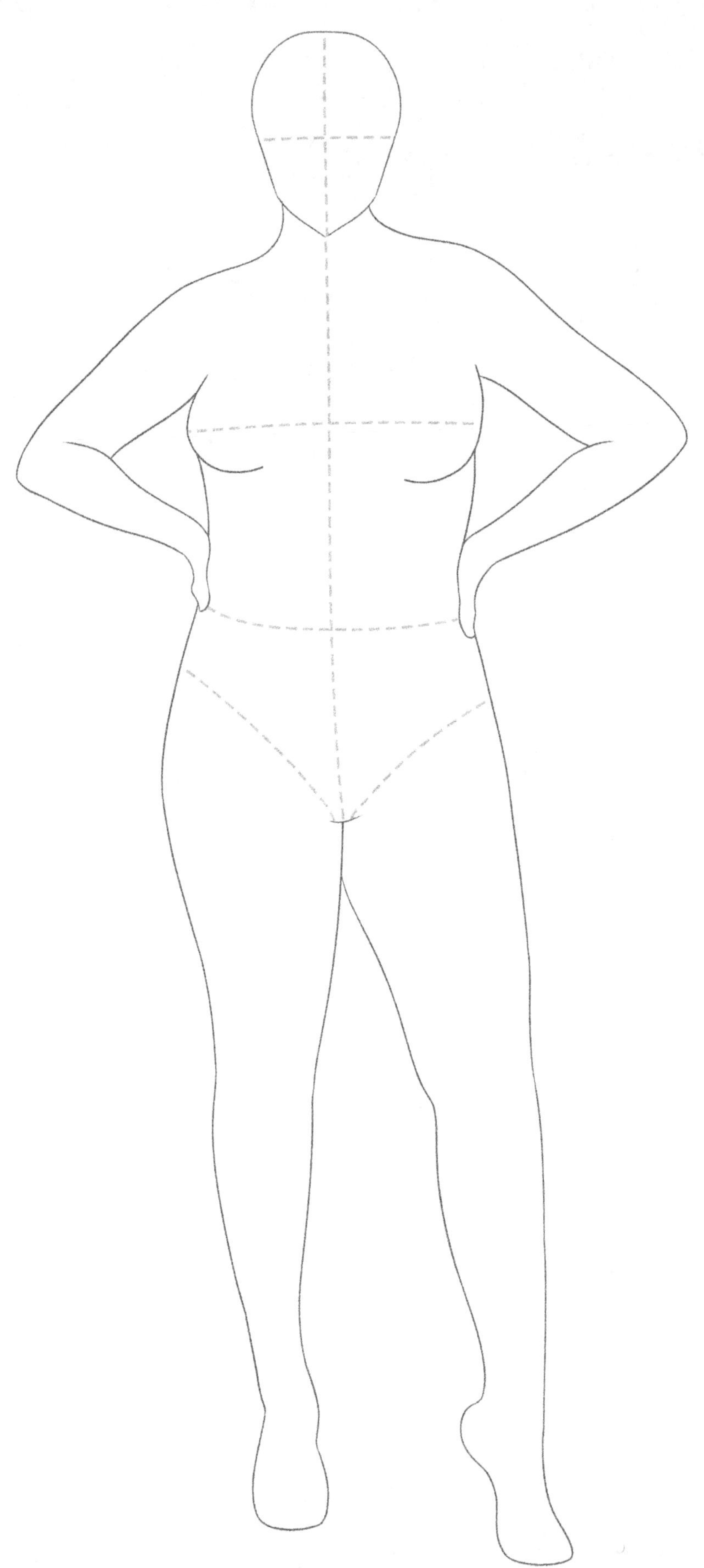

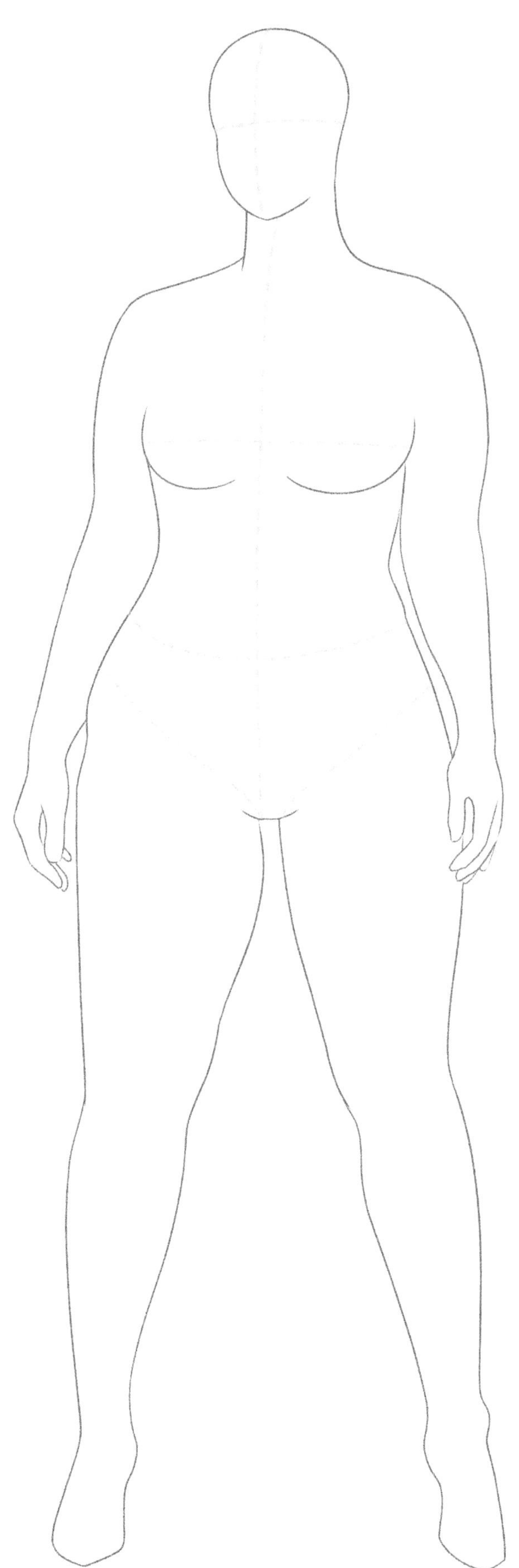

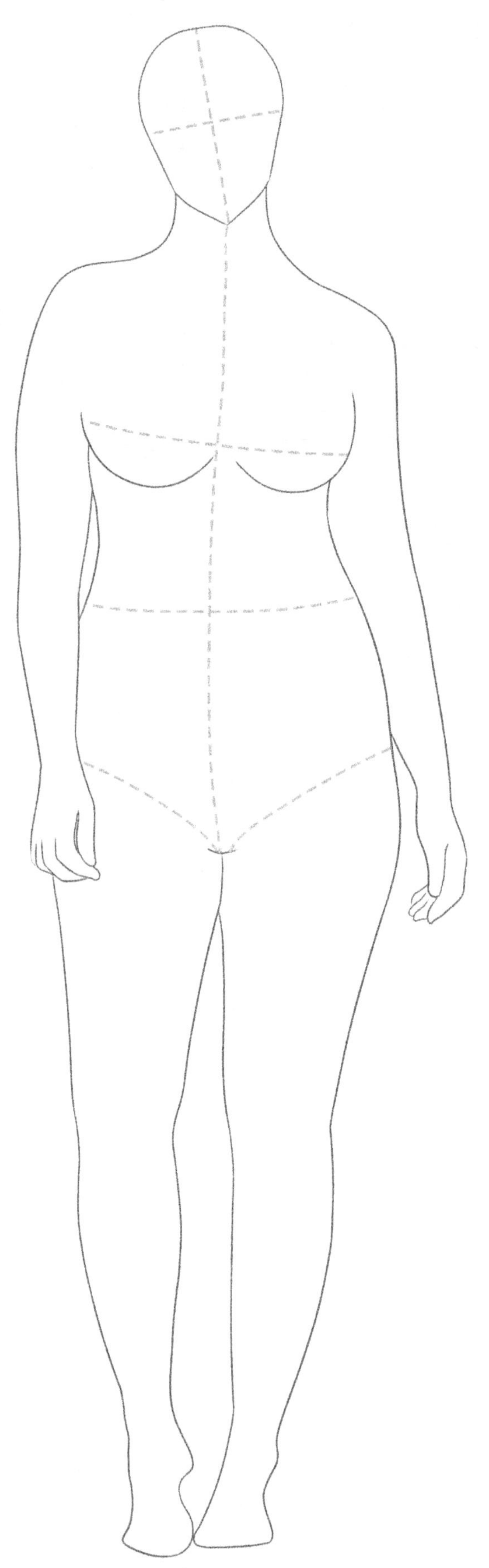

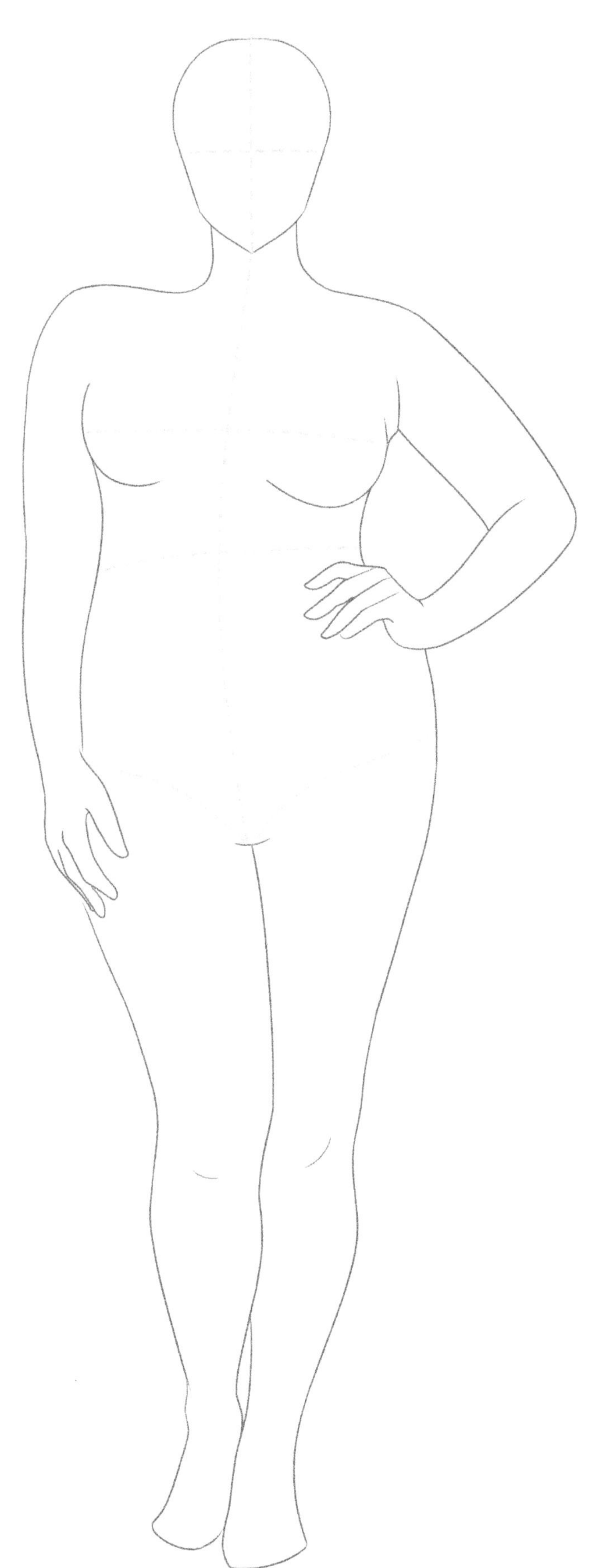

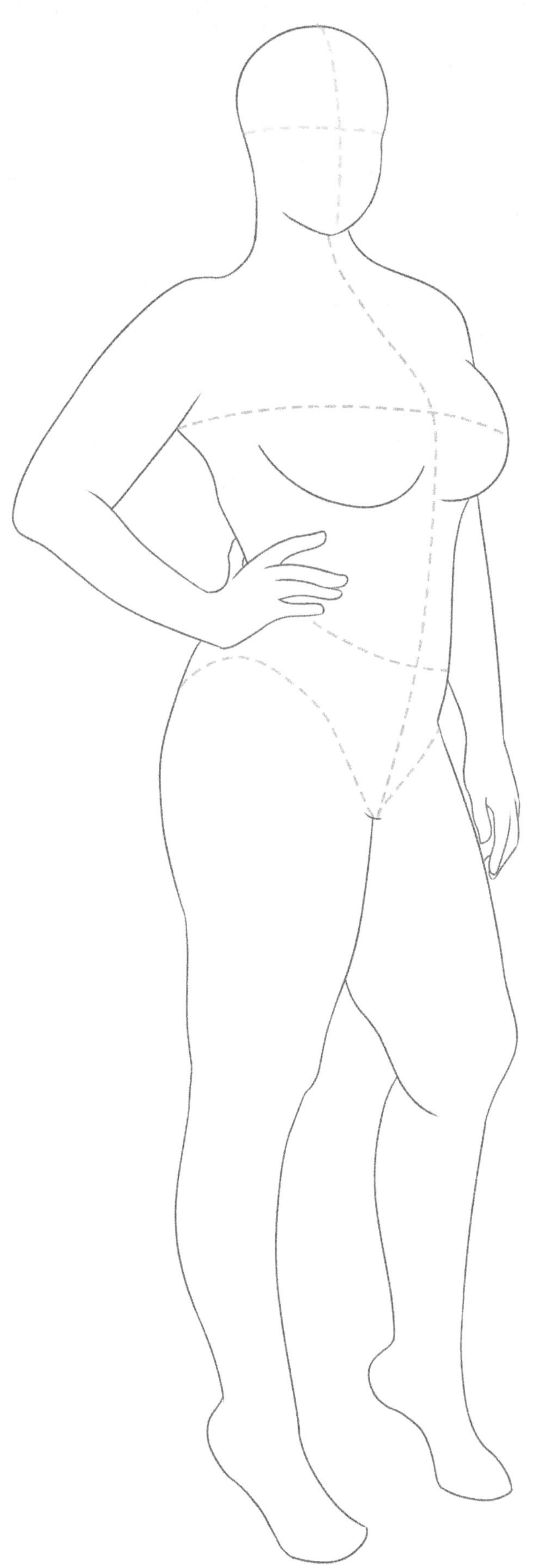

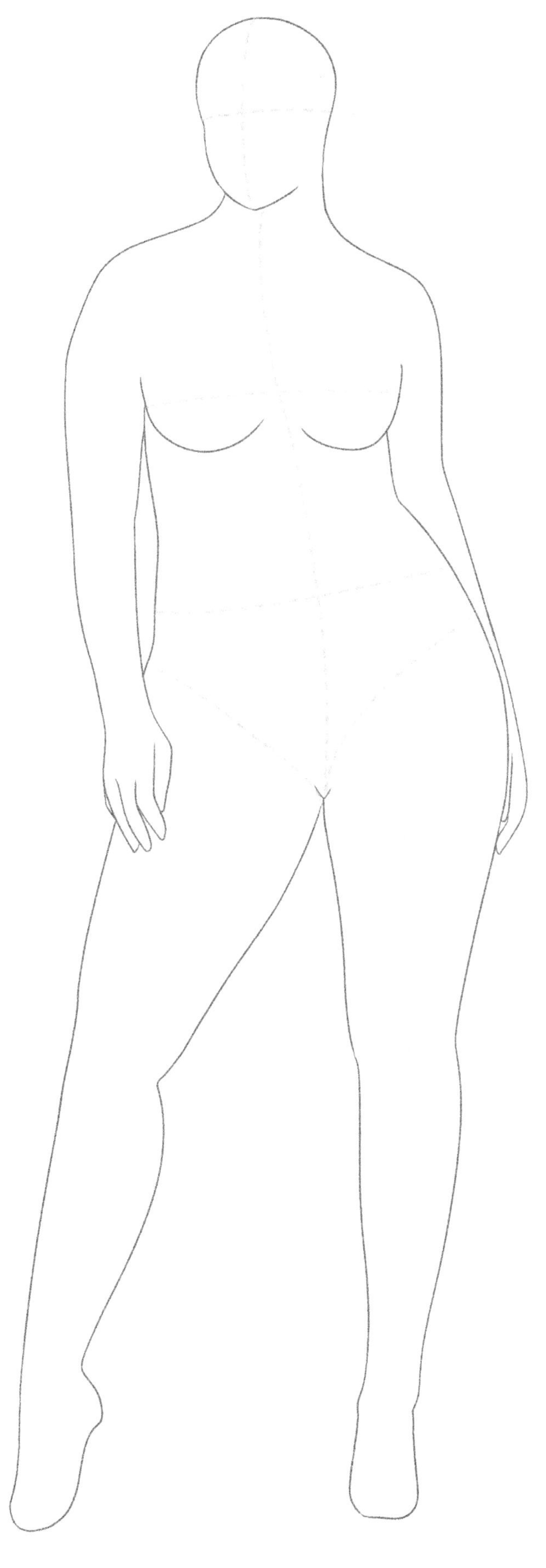

JOIN US AND GET 2 FASHION FIGURE TEMPLATES FOR FREE!

https://content.byebye.studio/designersupplynews

@_byebye_studio_

/byebyestudio

BYE
BYE
PAPER